Travels With Peppy

A Motorcycle Adventure Across the Country

42 States, 36 Days, & 10,188 Miles

by
Dean Stagg Lawrence

Copyright 1994 by Dean Lawrence

All rights reserved. No part of this book may be reproduced or transmitted in any form or by any means, electronic or mechanical, including photocopying, recording, or by any information storage or retrieval system without written permission from Triad Publishing, except for the inclusion of quotations in review, for which permission is granted.

Production by Gilliland Printing, Inc.
Copyediting by M. Carolyn Seigneur
Cover design by E.P. Puffin & Co.
Marketing by Word Services, Inc.

Travels With Peppy
A Motorcycle Adventure Across the Country
42 States, 36 Days, & 10,188 Miles

International Standard Book Number 0-9641348-0-2
Library of Congress Catalog Card Number 94-090172

Printed in the United States of America

Quantity Discounts are available from the publisher:
Triad Publishing
P.O. Box 412
Parker, Co. 80134

phone (303) 841-7265

For
my dear wife, Sandy, without whose ongoing support and encouragement this book, and indeed this journey, would not have been possible,

And also,
for those GoldWing riders all over the country who wish that they, too, could have experienced this adventure.

CONTENTS

Preface 9

Getting Ready 13

Day 1: Leaving Colorado 22

Day 2: South Dakota-Badlands 32

Day 3: Wyoming 44

Day 4: Yellowstone 54

Day 5: Lewis & Clark Trail 66

Day 6: Washington & Oregon 77

Day 7: Reno 89

Day 8: California Route 395 99

Day 9: Death Valley 107

Day 10: Arizona   117

Day 11: Reunion at Raton   125

Day 12: New Mexico   133

Day 13: Texas   141

Day 14: Oklahoma   151

Day 15: Arkansas   159

Day 16: Louisiana   167

Day 17: Alabama   175

Day 18: Florida   183

Day 19: Georgia & Carolinas 191

Day 20: Virginia   201

Day 21: More Virginia   207

Day 22: The Skyline Drive   215

Day 23: D.C., Md.& Delaware 223

Day 24: New Jersey   231

Day 25: Connecticut   237

Day 26: Massachusetts   245

Day 27: Maine   249

Day 28: N.H. & Vermont   255

Day 29: New York   261

Day 30: Pennsylvania   265

Day 31: Ohio & Kentucky   269

Day 32: Indiana & Illinois   273

Day 33: Missouri   277

Day 34: Kansas   281

Day 35: Western Kansas   283

Day 36: Colorado Homecoming 289

Travel Companion and Hunter.

The Hunted!

PREFACE

Why would any reasonably intelligent, fairly successful, non-skitzoid man of 49 years age want to leave the relative comfort of home and family to travel around the country on a motorcycle, towing a camper trailer and faithful canine companion named Peppy? The truth is... probably for the same reasons men have climbed mountains as far away as Tibet, dived to explore coral reefs under the sea, and ridden horses to remote wilderness regions: for the pure uncertain adventure of doing something entirely different from what most of us do between 9 and 5 every day.

I first started thinking about such an adventure when my wife and I attended the "Rally in the Rockies" at Estes Park, Colorado, toward the end of August, 1993. I had recently lost my job of three years, and, after a suitable period of obligatory mourning over not going to an office every day (and sometimes well into the night), it occurred to me there might be better things to do anyway.

The business machine industry is one of intense competition. Most of the independent dealers, including the one I worked for, are grossly undercapitalized, operating on float and hopes of float (interim cash in the bank after checks are written but before they are paid). Nevertheless, my employer, son of the founder, purchased a trendy loft, a new Mercedes, and gave himself a 40% raise, none of which was in the budget.

Yet it was my solemn responsibility to balance the Cash-Flow, i.e. collect the accounts receivables, pay all the bills on time, and meet payroll twice a month for 36 employees. Lots of pressure, long hours, very little monetary compensation, almost no support from the owners, even less recognition, this was the workplace.... Why am I sorry I don't have this job any longer?

So there we are, my wife and I in Estes Park at the Rally in the Rockies, when this man arrived on a large Suzuki Cavalcade touring bike (almost a Goldwing), towing a cargo trailer with his golden retreiver perched on top behind a crudely mounted windshield. The dog was lying down on a piece of thick carpeting, thoroughly enjoying the attention of all the passers-by, including us... well, mostly me.

What an intriguing idea I thought to myself: exploring new frontiers, braving the unknown with your dog *and* your motorcycle at the same time. I had always supposed that the two were mutually exclusive by reason of physical limitations: dogs don't sit on motorcycle seats (usually), and going for a ride in the truck, while often quite practical, as well as interesting and fun, especially for the dog, is just not the same level of exhiliration or exposure as a motorcycle trip. That particular rig, however, permitted only short trips because the dog was pretty much out in the open and had practically no protection at all in the event of a sudden stop, sideswipe, rain, or strangers. And then, of course, there was always the S.P.C.A. to surely protest such riding arrangements for the dog. My idea, actually my wife's idea, was to mount a Porta-Kennel, similar to the type required by airlines when shipping pets, on top of the trailer and train Peppy to jump in and out on command, when I opened the wire grate door. Since

Preface

Peppy is a Border Collie who had already proven himself a top quintile learner with extensive other obedience and working dog training, that is precisely the way my dream developed into reality.

But I am ahead of myself. As much as the idea of a 5-6 week cross country adventure excited me, ruining my marriage, or even adding a quantum dose of strain to it, was not an acceptable trade off. Either my dear wife willingly said it was okay with her and with us, or I would not proceed with the plan and the journey. After a tearful night of soul searching, followed by a reaffirmation of our mutual love and respect, Sandy gave me her pre-requisite approval for the trip, which included an absence of several weeks. I truly loved her all the more for this totally unselfish show of confidence and commitment in me. Now I could get on with the adventure of a lifetime. Whee....!

Rally in the Rockies, Estes Park

Sandy and I, touring.

GETTING READY

Once the emotional decision had been made, I was committed to the adventure of my life! Peppy and I were going to ride like the wind (within the speed limits, of course) through 42 states. We would camp, sightsee, meet new people and sniff new sniffs. But first, there were details - big details. Time was of the essence. Could I physically be ready in two weeks? In Colorado where we lived, we had already tasted cold weather in the foothills and snow, more than once, in the High Country. If I could not leave before the end of September, I would not be able to cross the entire United States due to the cold (forget comfort). Having grown up in New England, I knew that fall came early to Maine, New Hampshire, and Vermont, the last northern segment of my trip. It was risky anyway weather-wise at this time of year, but if I was not through New England by the middle of October, I'd be just begging for trouble. Stories of other riders in heavy rain, pounding hail, even snow, and ice like a bobsled run, did not excite me; they were foolhardy. I did not mind being courageous, but I didn't want to be stupid. The Motorcycle Safety Foundation course we had taken a few months ago left several indelible impressions on me: ride within your limits, don't take chances with safety, and always think "What could happen if...?" Those lessons would serve me well through 42 states and 10,188 miles. Safety was number 1. It had to be.

My first challenge was to find a camper trailer I could rent or purchase to pull behind my GoldWing. My own Chapter J of the Colorado GoldWing Road Riders Association was having their regular monthly meeting in only 2 days where I could plead my case to see if anyone knew someone who had such a trailer they were not using right now, wanted to sell, would rent, etc. In the meantime, I called all the different manufacturers advertised in the *WingWorld* and *Rider* magazines. They referred me to their area representatives and dealers. Actually, I spent most of that Tuesday on the phone. My search for a trailer, available now, was on in earnest. All the manufacturers, about 5 or 6 from California to Pennsylvania, were more than happy to order a trailer for me, customize it to my specifications, and ship it to Colorado by Thanksgiving, for $3000 to $5000. Of course, there were two conflicting limitations: time and money.

A couple of dealers had motorcycle campers in stock, so I browsed in an attempt to learn more about trailers and their relative costs before evaluating my current options. Two different dealers had trailers for sale, but they looked rather awkward to me. Setting them up "just took a little getting used to...you'll have no trouble once you're out on the road." That's what I was afraid of - trouble out on the road - and was still unconvinced.

Luck was really with me now, however, at the next GWRRA Chapter J meeting. I shared my search efforts with the group and described my plans. Two different members had camper/trailers they wanted to sell. Both were in excellent condition and much cleaner than those for sale from the dealer or manufacturer's rep. As it turned out, the family of Chapter J's Area Representative, Larry Cutsinger, had previously been involved in motorcycle trailer manufacturing back in Indiana. He currently had three trailers, one cargo and two campers, at his home in Colorado.

Full of anticipation, actually my wife's anticipation was 50% anxiety, we visited Larry the next night for a "demonstration." He and his wife made it look kindergarten-simple to set up the camper rig:... "just insert this pole here, lift the top onto the poles, raise it all up with the frame, and presto, you have your tent ready for sleeping, reading, and eating." (I tried to remember those words on my first night in western Nebraska when howling winds at 30 m/p/h made me stumble like a drunk as I wrestled those same poles, tenting canvas, and top, wondering if I was going to make it through two states much less forty or so).

Larry and Ilona's demonstration convinced me and, not only was this camper easy to use, it was beautiful. The shade of blue did not exactly match my Honda Aspencade, but it was a good blend and made an eye-catching combination, even before I added the silver lettering, "Travels With Peppy," and the dog kennel. The paint had a rich glossy finish that almost demanded you wipe off your fingerprints after touching it. All the materials were first-class, especially the aluminum body, which was solid and rigid, yet only a third of the weight of steel. I was impressed with the quality of the construction. Even the inside had thick, well-upholstered cushions for sitting and sleeping. A solid, well-varnished Birch plywood pedestal doubled as a table top and bed frame section. This was not exactly a room at the Hilton, but I was sure it would meet my needs for a long journey, and would accommodate

Peppy without a motel manager's judgmental glance. We would be on our own; independent, just as I wanted.

Now we move onto that other limitation: money. I shared my planned budget for the trip with Larry. "Just tell me how you'd like to work it out and I'll go along with you if at all possible," he said. True to his word, he agreed to a lease/purchase contract with an option for me to buy the trailer after I got back from the trip, if I wanted to, with full credit for the payments already made. I could not have asked for a more flexible agreement and made sure he and his wife understood how much I appreciated their credit and confidence.

Then came one of many great surprises on this adventure. While contemplating the trailer hooked up to my big motorcycle, Larry's wife, Ilona, asked, "Can I come along? It's my kind of trip and you are going to have an extra seat anyway." I hardly knew what to say or how to say it. "What about your family and work obligations?" I stammered, trying to avoid the other more personal problems such travel arrangements would present.

"Oh, they'll still be here when I get back" she said, and then, she laughed. And so did I, a big nervous laugh of relief to know we were all just kidding.

Then, out comes Larry who, in addition to everything he was already doing for me, offers to install the wiring harness which connects my GL1200's running and brake lights to the trailer. We shook hands on the deal, I drew up a contract with the help of a PC software program called "It's Legal", and made arrangements to pick up the trailer the following week.

Next, I bought a Markland receiver hitch from the local Honda dealer, spent a few hours on my back threading bolts where I didn't even know there were any, and, when the aching went away, returned to my friend for the wiring harness work. After a few minor hiccups with the brake lights not working on either the bike or the trailer, we got everything together. I was on my way home with a beautiful sparkling rig any middle aged vagabond would be proud to show off around the country.

But time was running short now. A previously scheduled business trip to Atlanta (via airplane) had consumed three of my precious remaining days. Only six left and lots of details to take care of.

It was very important that I write my parents and brothers, all of whom live back East, what my plans were so they would not collapse in shock if and when I showed up at their respective doorsteps on a motorcycle they didn't even know I owned. Actually, this was my fourth motorcycle, but the last one was over 15 years ago, so this was not exactly current on their minds as my chief recreational activity, much less a cross country conveyance! I was especially concerned that my 75 year-old mother have "thought time" to put this whole journey in perspective. When I got my first motorcycle, at age 17, she cried for hours over the certainty of my imminent death; not just dying quietly in my sleep mind you, but rather a sudden knocking at the door by a policeman with dreadful news of a fatal accident, asking would she please come down to the morgue to identify what was left of any body parts she thought had been mine. This image has only slightly mitigated over the last 32 years, but I am grateful for small progress. So when she called, after receiving the letter outlining my trip plans, I was genuinely relieved that there was no weeping and gnashing of teeth. On the contrary, after my dear wife got through relating her own conversion from thinking (and fearing) the same flesh searing notions about motorcycling as my mother, only to be born again with wonderful enjoyment of the great outdoors, taking exhilarating trips into the mountains of Colorado, to the mesas of New Mexico, plus scenic Wyoming, etc., well... you could just sense that my mother had an inner peace never before contemplated.

The next most important preparation had to do with money. During my previous employment I had squirreled away some funds for my retirement in a 401K plan. Since I had lost my job for reasons other than my own choosing, this was almost like being retired, and I really needed a couple of thousand dollars to "invest" in what was to be the excursion of a lifetime and which would surely provide the subject matter for a New York Times bestseller. My budget plan was to spend $12 per day on fuel, 2 tankfuls, $6 on campsites, and $12 on food, total: $30 per day. Since I thought it would take about 35 days @ an average of 300 miles per day, that would require $1050 out of pocket. $2000 should give me plenty of leeway for overages or unplanned expenses to say nothing of outright frivolous purchases, which, on rare moments of weakness, I have from time to time been known to make. Of course, there was always the additional comfort of a fortified plastic card in my wallet just waiting to be embossed in any of the 40 states not yet having shown up on my Visa statement.

Then there was the matter of additional insurance. When we bought the motorcycle several months ago, I told our insurance agent we were only going to be riding it on the weekends during the summer. Therefore, we purchased only the minimum liability insurance to be legal. Much to my surprise, this coverage was only $65. After a few months of riding, especially taking some of the three and four day excursions GWRRA chapters are famous for, we decided to add a Comprehensive Coverage clause, just in case the bike was stolen or vandalized, another $109. Now that I was also going to use a trailer that was not even mine, and since the owner had said he did not have any current insurance coverage, I talked to our agent again about collision insurance for the bike and trailer, add on $159. I have never figured out whether the insurance bills are worse than the actual losses, but at least there is that ever elusive peace of mind. You're broke, but your mind is at ease.

Time is flying by now, and only three days before blast off. I decided early on that this might well be my lifetime adventure and anything I could do to help document the activity would be helpful. Therefore, with all the lettering on the sides of the trailer and the kennel, which fit perfectly on top of the trailer between the side rails, I took off for the mountains with Peppy for a trial run and some picture taking. Since there was only one of me, and since it is not wise to always count on the assistance of a passing tourist to help out with the pressing of an exposure button on a camera, I purchased a collapsible tripod on which I could mount the camera, set the timer, and execute self-photography. Strange as it may seem, it worked perfectly. The result was a dramatic pose of Peppy and me with the GoldWing and trailer, all in front of Lake Dillon at the I-70 scenic rest area near Silverthorn. The shot turned out so well that I had a hundred copies made and gave them out to different people in every state during the trip as a memento. Usually, it was also a thank you for hospitality or courtesy at the time, always well received with only one exception in Virginia, which I will mention later.

It is down to the wire now, and go time is tomorrow. Final errands include buying a piece of carpet to glue onto the top of the Igloo cooler, which sits in a frame holder in front of the trailer body. Peppy was slipping when he tried to jump up to his kennel, and I thought the all-weather carpet would give him more traction. Another really pleasant surprise: the very first carpet dealer I called on loved Border Collies and would not think of *selling* me a little square, "Here take as many as you want of these discontinued colors, no charge". She meant it too, *free*. One of the shades of gray matched the color of the cooler perfectly, so with a little trim and a lot of contact cement, Peppy had a very functional bounding board which proved to be his prime opportunity to show off almost every day of the entire trip. People would ask "How does he like traveling in his kennel?" and I would say, "Pep...Hup... Hup," and he'd jump up on the cooler top and into his kennel, less than two seconds elapsed time. Then he would bathe in the shower of affection bestowed on him by the curious and impressionable tourists. He loved being the center of attention and got more than his share of it over the next 5 weeks.

End of the errands; last minute check list (there's a really good one in the Gold Book, but I couldn't understand why they question if my will was up to date). Going to sleep Friday night was difficult. Fitful turns and another look at the clock...still only 4 a.m. Can't get up until at least 5, after all, she is my wife.

A final cup of coffee!

Leaving home, September 25th.

Day 1: LEAVING COLORADO

Saturday, September 25, 1993, was a beautiful, crisp, clear day - the kind Colorado is famous for. The radio said the temperature was 48 degrees Farenheit in Denver but our thermometer in Parker read only 39 at 6 a.m. No matter. The sun was already peaking over the horizon in a sure and welcomed process of warming everything up, including me. Breakfast was hurried; there was no sense in dragging out the good-byes. All had been said and this was the time I had spent so many hours and days planning for. The bike sparkled; it was cleaner than it would be for almost two months, and I had hooked up the trailer before breakfast.

Peppy was acting a bit strangely, however. Normally, when we first get up in the morning, he has a little urge for wanderlust, often preferring to scout around the house and neighborhood, checking out the other dogs' food dishes before returning for his own breakfast. No wandering this morning! He was glued to the motorcycle and trailer in the driveway. Even as he saluted a favorite bush nearby, he cocked his head toward me so that he could constantly keep his eyes on all the preparation activity. He knew something was happening real close to "GO," a word he had learned as a pup, and this dog was not going to be left behind. It was against his instincts, background, experience, training, and even religion, to lay back when there was any activity, much less "GO" time. This was prime time for him.

"Let's go. Hup, hup,"and that's all she wrote. Peppy had jumped into his kennel via the cooler and settled onto his lambskin-covered bed, smiling and relieved that this was going to be *his* trip too. Sandy took a picture of us at the top of the driveway, with the sun behind her casting shadows everywhere. It later became one of my favorite pictures from the entire journey, with the bright sun contrasting the dark motorcycle and trailer against the shimmering trees and concrete driveway. Another kiss and a hug for the road, and we were off on the adventure of a lifetime!

Going down Thunderbird Road, heading out of the Pinery residential area where we lived, I could already see the golfers lined up on the first hole, waiting for their pre-assigned tee times and their chance to belt one out down the fairway. While normally I like to play golf as much as the next fellow, maybe even more when I'm hitting my irons well, this morning was different. I felt almost sorry for those guys whose high point of the whole day would be that game, or even one hole, maybe even one shot where that little ball cooperated and stopped on the green or dropped into the hole. This was a day of high adventure for Peppy and me, no time for mundane activity like golf.

As we turned onto Colorado State Highway 83, our first big problem with the weather became apparent. The sun was very bright for early in the morning, but because we were heading south, I could turn my helmet, with visor, a little to the left and block it out. However, when we turned east on Highway 86 at Franktown, it was a different story. Now I was heading directly into the rising sun, and it was blinding.

Should I pull off the road after only five miles? What if someone I knew stopped to see if I was all right on my great big trip, before I even got six miles from home? All the members from the Parker Rotary Club had given me a warm and gallant send off two days earlier, at the regular Thursday morning meeting, and many of the Rotarians lived all around this area. I could not bear the thought of such disgrace. There was no stopping now.

    My Shoei helmet had a visor which extended about two inches and allowed for at least a little bit of artificial shade. As I looked down at the road, I could see about twenty feet in front of the bike before the sun's glare hit me straight in the eyes blinding any more forward vision. I slowed down to about 40 miles per hour and was blessed with the appearance of a farm truck hauling a tall load of hay and going only 35 miles per hour. He became my slow-poke excuse; I stayed behind him all the way to Kiowa, about 15 miles, much to the dismay of the drivers behind me. I would have been happy to pull off if it was just Peppy and me slowing them down, but I really needed the truck's load of hay to block the sun when we went around those gradual curves. The hay truck turned off as we reached the edge of town, and was good timing. I was ready for our first real stop.

    It had been only been 30 minutes since leaving home, but I was ready for a second cup of coffee and a chance to think things out. Had I forgotten anything reallly essential? Was Peppy having any problems? Would anybody in Kiowa ask about my trip? Did *they* know where I was going? Did *I* know where I was going? Did *anybody* care? The answers were "no" on almost all counts.

At this short distance from home, there was no need to refuel the GoldWing, but I needed that cup of coffee. And the only place serving coffee on Saturday morning in Kiowa was a Conoco station that happened to be down to the last drop before I got my cup. The older man at the cash register thanked me for letting him know they were out and offered a reduced-price donut while I waited for a new pot to brew. He grumbled about the last customers not even telling him they had taken the last of the coffee, like it was their job to keep him informed on the coffee pot status. Then there was that ubiquitous subject which would come up daily over the entire country...the weather.

"Pretty nippy out there on a motorcycle, eh?"

"Yeah, sure is, but looks like it'll warm up before too long."

"Don't know. They're calling for a storm toward Limon this afternoon."

"That's where I'm heading, and from there, up to Nebraska."

"Well, you'd better keep an eye out for the weather."

I didn't have the heart to tell the old man that you don't have any choice on a touring motorcycle; you're always watching the weather. The coffee was good, and as a harbinger of the entire trip, Peppy made friends quickly with customers who walked through the door while I was inside jawing with the manager.

A quick "Hup, hup" and we were on our way again, heading east on Highway 86 toward Limon. The sun had risen far enough in the sky over that last half hour to reduce the glare. It had dropped back to being a minor annoyance by 9:30 and no problem at all a little later.

Eastern Colorado is completely different from the western part of the state. No mountains here at all, just rolling hills turning into less rolling hills before becoming just plain flat land, with an occasional rise or fall to the horizon. Colorado Highway 86 intersected with I-70 about 10 miles before Limon; we followed it into town before heading straight north on Colorado Highway 71, toward Ft. Morgan, about 85 miles distant. My travel plan was to stay off the interstates whenever possible for two main reasons. One, I generally find the secondary roads more interesting with their little towns, roadside shops, and varied scenery. Two, I also hate competing with big tractor trailer trucks for "position." It's not that I want their lane or even their speed, it's just that when you're on two wheels, pulling a trailer, a truck passing you at 80 miles per hour really blows you around. Of course, a 1200cc Honda GoldWing can go 80 miles per hour too, or, for that matter, even 100 miles per hour, but it's not a comfortable cruising speed, nor is it legal. The truckers have their job to do, which usually means getting some cargo to its destination in the shortest possible time. My job was to really see as much as possible and forget speed records. So I generally left the interstates to the trucks, a little known fact for which I'm sure they were wholeheartedly grateful. (Later, at some of the truck stops, I chatted with a quite a few drivers and was surprised to learn they were pretty decent human beings; people you would never suspect of having homicidal tendencies, even toward motorcyclists.)

Forty miles north of Limon is the first town on Highway 71. Appropriately called "Last Chance," it was a crossroads town where there used to be a gas station of sorts, years ago, but there was no activity now. Wonder what it used to be the "last chance" for? Gas? Water? I was glad I had topped off the fuel tank in Limon, after seeing Last Chance and the mileage sign to Ft.Morgan (47 miles). I could feel a storm starting to brew with the winds picking up as we went north. Ft. Morgan was about 10 miles west of the intersection of Highway 71 and I-76, heading northeast toward Sterling, my next stop. At this point I was ready to take on the big highway - I, too, needed to make some time in order to reach Chadron, Nebraska before nightfall.

A few miles north of Sterling, we crossed into Nebraska, and the weather seemed to worsen almost immediately. The light breezes turned into heavier winds, and I found myself wondering how long I could ride keeled over at what seemed like a 30-degree angle. Sidney, Nebraska was a welcomed stop not only for the rest, but also for a chance to wander through Cabella's, the giant sporting goods and camping store. There are always things you could buy in that kind of place- another sweater, more warm socks, another pair of jeans with flannel linings, or even a face mask for those really cold days ahead. Practicality, however, lost out to a trail blazer's fancy. I bought one of those portable diamond-crusted knife sharpeners that will put a razor's edge on anything that is supposed to cut. It came in a leather carrying case, too, which made it irresistible for anyone (like me) on a camping adventure. That was my logic and justification for that $30, another absolutely necessary expense.

A few miles west of Sidney, we picked up Nebraska Highway 385, a road we would head north on for the last 135 miles of our first day. If the wind had been blowing before, it was really coming across the high plains now, mixed with light rain, and made the trip to the L & V campground in Chadron an hour longer.

A very nice lady named Vera (surely the "V" of "L & V Campground") came out to check me in and bear the bad tidings; it was supposed to be windy, rainy, and cold tonight. Great, I thought. I could hardly wait. The good news, however, was that their fee for "Tent Campers" was only $4, which included use of the community bathroom. "If you get too cold," she said, "you can come in here and sleep on the couch. It's not much, but it'll be warmer than outside. The dog's okay, too." I thanked her for the genuine concern but assured her that Peppy and I would be fine outside in the camper.

Was I lying to her, to myself? How much cold could I really stand? I absolutely did not know, but the thought of not being able to spend even the first night in the camper was more than my pride would allow. By this time I was more anxious about setting up camp since the wind was blowing harder already, and it was almost dark. Much to my relief, neither Vera nor her assistant stood around to watch me set up the camper tent, a task at which I would soon be an old hand at, but wasn't yet.

There were many sites available so I rode the bike to the closest one, shielded by the building, where I hoped the wind would break up a bit. The ground was nice and level with some gravel for solid footings. After unhooking Peppy's kennel and setting it on the ground, I pulled the spring-loaded stabilizer jacks down in the back, lowered the telescoping jack in front, and popped the top off. The solid birch plywood flaps folded out butterfly-style with metal support rods to keep them from bending too far toward the ground. The wooden flaps were perfectly parallel, so far so good. Aluminum poles inside the camper went into vertical tubes which would then hold up the top of the trailer, which also contained the tenting and made up the walls and door of the camper. I could hardly stand up with the top in my arms. The wind was blowing so hard, it forced me to my knees more than once. However, after a half hour of wrestling, the rig was assembled. The other piece of Birch plywood went across the middle of the trailer, inside, and made a platform on which I placed the big three inch thick cushions that became my mattress. Finally, I laid the sleeping bag across the makeshift bed and there it was, my home for tonight.

It was completely dark now, and both Peppy and I were ready for dinner, wind or not. His was easy to get out of the large trailer-frame cooler, along with his small insulated water container, which traveled inside. The top of his little cooler also doubled as his food dish, and I had bought a dozen packs of dry Moist & Meaty which suited him just fine. Fine, that is, until I started to eat my fried chicken which I had bought at the last gas stop in Chadron. Sucker that I am, Peppy got the skins and gristle before we both turned in, stomachs full and dog tired. (He had had a strenuous couple of hours chasing all the pesky squirrels up their trees in the two acres of campground before dinner.)

That night was anything but restful. When calling Sandy to say everything was fine on my first day ride of 426 miles, I couldn't bear to tell her how horrible the windy Nebraska segment had actually been. It would just cause her to worry more than she already was about this whole excursion. That night, sure enough, the wind blew even harder, and it rained buckets at timely intervals just to complete the right atmosphere for a first night of camping. Although I hate to admit it, I lay there wondering if I should turn around tomorrow and head back to Denver. Of course, I would be considered the biggest wimp in the whole state, the Rotary Club would probably disbar me, and my kids would say, "It's all right, Dad" while inside I knew they would really be pondering why I had no guts anymore. My wife, of course, would be relieved to see me home safe. No, I decided. I could not turn around. I had to push on. My ego would not let me entertain that thought any longer, and that's all there was to it. Such was the courage demonstrated the first day out. Peppy had a field day, and I licked my psychological wounds, full of apprehension about tomorrow.

First night in Nebraska.

Peppy wins campground
frisbee contest!

Day 2: SOUTH DAKOTA- BADLANDS

Finally, the next morning, the sun came up. Low and behold, it had stopped raining, but the wind was still gusting about 20 knots, interspersed with periods of relative calm. I took advantage of those to break camp. Everything folded up more quickly this morning than it had unfolded the night before. The tenting was damp but, as I learned later, the quality of the 420 denier pack cloth was good enough to allow it to stay wet for two to three days without any harmful effects, like mildew.

Just as Peppy was ready to jump into his kennel, a neighboring camper approached with Pep's frisbee. (He had dropped it in the dark last night.)

"Where you headed today?" he asked.

"Going up to South Dakota, through the Badlands and on to Mt. Rushmore," I said.

"If you mean the *real* Badlands that will be a good bit out of your way from Mt. Rushmore. Let me show you on a map."

Sure enough, he was right. It was at least 70 miles from Mt. Rushmore to the Badlands National Park Visitor Center. I had always thought that all of western South Dakota was "The Badlands," but being from North Dakota,, my neighbor set me straight, which I appreciated. He then told me that he was semi-retired, but that his hobby and second income was playing a clarinet in a band. He had just come from a gig in Scottsbluff, and he and his wife were "camping their way back home." This was the first of what seemed like a hundred retired couples I would meet on this trip who liked camping around the country. His particular rig was only a shell on the back of his pickup truck, with an elevated top and a rear door. They had a little kitchen for "every now and then", but mainly he and the missis ate out and used the camper only for sleeping. This was among the most modest of the retiree RV rigs I would see on my campground excursions.

I thanked my neighbor for his travel advice, the wayward frisbee, and waved goodbye just as he was taking another deep breath. I had the feeling we could have stayed there all day talking about what we wanted to do and where we wanted to go.

The road from Chadron was a continuation of Highway 385 heading north. In less than 20 miles we were crossing into South Dakota. As with most of the states, a big "Welcome" sign from the governor greeted us at the state line. Maybe it was just my imagination, but the wind seemed to die down as soon as we crossed the line and by the time we reached Hot Springs, another 30 miles, it was as pretty a fall day as any biker could ask for- crisp and cool with sunshine and visibility that went on for miles.

Since neither Peppy nor I had eaten breakfast, Hot Springs was definitely going to be a food stop. However, 9 a.m. Sunday morning is not when most restaurants are open, at least not in Hot Springs. Finally, as we were leaving town, and running out of choices, we found the Braun Hotel, a big, old gothic structure alive with people milling about the huge porchway near the main entrance.

The hotel was built into the side of a mountain which rose hundreds of feet behind the building itself, and looked like giant stair stepping stones to the brilliant blue sky. Like a lot of historic landmarks, circa 1903, big, old oak trees crowded the parking lot. Their acorns kept falling all over the ground and squirrels scampered back to their nests, hoarding their new found loot. All this activity was not lost on Peppy, who could hardly take time to eat his morning kibbles with all those little varmints he was keeping track of just in case I untied him later. He's never actually caught an animal, but he loves to try, and puts all his heart into those hell-bent-for-leather, zig-zag chases. But this time, the squirrels were safe, much to Peppy's chagrin.

Although people had been coming out of the Hotel Braun, there was nobody in the lobby at all, no customers and no employees. The front desk was empty, with notices on the bulletin board next to the counter outlining the special activities or just the "specials." One that intrigued me was the "free" use of the adjoining bath house and hot spring for guests of the hotel. If this had been the end of the day, instead of the beginning, I would have been tempted to soak my bones in that "world famous" hot bath and spend the night. As it was, however, breakfast was my main concern. About that time, a young man with a white apron on came out from another hallway over which was the sign, "Hotel Restaurant." I asked him if it were open for breakfast and, somewhat surprisingly, he said he didn't know but he would find out. A few minutes later he reappeared and confirmed that the restaurant was open and to please follow him. He lead me through a huge, empty dining room, and around another series of corners to a lunch counter with everything, stools, coffee pot, pie shelves, and more - except customers. It almost scares me a little when nobody else thinks this is the right time or place to have something to eat, but I was beyond other options now- I was hungry. The boy poured me a cup of coffee, gave me a menu, and went around the back of the wall into the kitchen. I could hear him ask his dad what to do next, and at that point, it all started to make sense to me. Dad was new himself at the cook job, his son was helping out, and the hotel had not built up any regular Sunday morning eatery clientele. Nevertheless, I had no complaints about the bacon and eggs, over easy, with an English muffin on the side. Even if I had really wanted a fancy breakfast, I would not have had the guts to order Eggs Benedict or Strawberry Crepes, both on the old, well-worn menu. Just the thought of spelling out the words to the neophyte waiter seemed cruel, and beyond the need for simple nourishment.

Just before my eggs arrived, without any fanfare or introduction, another customer walked in, asking the same questions I had about being open for breakfast, etc., and picks out a stool 2 or 3 down from where I was sitting. This guy is tall, thin, and unshaven for at least a couple of days. His clothes were soiled and dishelved while his light hiking boots were unlaced and untied. "Lester," I learned, was from New York City, owned a dry cleaning store on the West Side with a partner, and took a late summer vacation every year to go hiking and camping with his girlfriend for a week or so. Last year, they did Colorado and Rocky Mountain National Park. This year, they had just returned from Mt. Rushmore by way of Wyoming and Montana. He told me that in all honesty he had been a little disappointed with the granite carvings of the presidents because he thought they would be much bigger from all the pictures he had seen. When I asked where his girlfriend was, he said she was trying to put on her make-up before coming in for breakfast. I left a half hour later, and she still had not appeared. I guess her facial preparations were quite an ordeal. As I left, I wondered how they could have camped for a week in a tent with those kind of heavy-duty cosmetic requirements. Thankfully, in my wife's words, I come with a "Wash 'N Wear" face. Not much to it, to be sure, but at least it's ready to go after only a few minutes in the most spartan of rest rooms. Campgrounds are not famous for their elaborate bathroom facilities. Most of the time I was happy if I had toilet paper and a sit-down commode.

Leaving Hot Springs, we were headed north toward the Wind Cave National Park and Mt. Rushmore on South Dakota Highway 87. As we left town, I saw several construction signs but didn't pay much attention to them. (The entire country is under construction these days.) However, after a few turns up the mountain, I saw the reason for the signs. The road became sheer, nerve racking hell. The paving company had laid down the blacktop going south and left the north side of the road (my side) rough-graded gravel. There was about six inches actual difference in height between our gravel road and the paved lane going the other direction. The red cones and barricades completely separated the two directions, but the slope on our side tapered right to the edge of a cliff that scared the dickens out of me just to look at, much less drive. There was no place to pull off; I had no choice but to side-slip the bike and trailer for the next seven

South Dakota - Badlands

miles. Perhaps a car could have crawled along without any danger of falling off the edge, but this rider was genuinely afraid of turning a few hundred cartwheels before coming to rest at the bottom of some steep ravine where the boy scouts would hike upon my wreckage next Spring.

Fortunately, nothing like that happened. A good shower later that night cleaned the dried sweat off my back, and a washing machine took care of anything I left in my undershorts. This incident reminded me, however, of my instructor at one of the Motorcycle Safety Foundation classes who said that the Department of Highways, in most states, does not feel it is necessary for roads under construction to meet *motorcycle* safety standards. If they're good enough for four wheels, they say, that takes care of most of the taxpaying public.

Wind Cave National Park almost made the gravel-slide nightmare worthwhile. Herds of buffalo roamed the grass praires with complete disregard for me or the bike and trailer. I couldn't see Peppy directly from my saddle, but my guess is his eyes were wide open when those huge animals skirted the road, breathing a natural snort like some pre-historic monsters out of the Ice Age from eons past. Just as when a bike approaches a strange dog, my strategy was to be ready to accelerate lickety-split if any of the bison charged us on the paved roadway. Even with the trailer on back, I knew the GoldWing could get me out of harm's way, a feeling I have grown to value on more than one occasion.

In addition to the Bison herds, there were graceful antelope almost flowing across the grassy hills. One of my favorite animals, though, was the plentiful prairie dog. I do not know at what point a prairie dog becomes a ground hog, but these fellas must have been trying to qualify. They were big, fat, and full of squeaks and squeals when I let Peppy out to round up a few. He had a grand time chasing them into their burrowed holes, but as soon as one dived for cover, his brothers were up on sentry duty screeching the alarm for the rest of the pack. The park was almost empty (of humans) by the end of September, so I took some liberties which would not have been proper in the middle of summer. (After Labor Day, all the national parks and campgrounds have one third the number of visitors compared to peak summer months.)

Nevertheless, Mt. Rushmore had a good crowd, and if mid-summer was three times this number of tourists, the Visitors Center and parking lot traffic jams must rival Times Square. There were a lot of buses with foreign tourists, one loaded with Australians who could not get enough of Peppy, his travel accommodations, and, to a lesser extent, his chauffeur. We posed for pictures, took some of them with Peppy, and the bike, and more. When the bus driver unceremoniously yelled that the bus was leaving, the chorus of moans and groans was almost embarassing to me. Almost. I loved it as much as Peppy did, even though he always got more hugs.

No sooner had this wonderful, sensitive, and intelligent group left than a fellow from Arkansas ambled over and asked Peppy's name. Surely he was putting me on, I thought. Peppy and I were sitting on the grass right next to the bike. "Travels With Peppy" was obvious on both sides of the trailer, with "Peppy" stenciled onto his kennel in eight inch letters. I looked him straight in the eye, told him politely, "Peppy." He

South Dakota - Badlands

said, "Oh yea", and kept on up the path to the visitor center. I am not making light of people from Arkansas; I saw the plates on his car when he got out next to us in the parking lot.

The granite sculptures at Mt. Rushmore were smaller than I thought they would be, each head about 60 feet high, but since Lester had already shared his opinions with me, I was expecting it and not disappointed. Far more impressive than the shere dimensions, however, was the philosophy put forth by the man who had chiseled away at this rock from 1927 to 1941:

> "A monument's dimensions shall be determined by the importance to civilization of the events commemorated...Let us place there, carved high, as close to heaven as we can,...our leaders, their faces, to show posterity what manner of men they were.Then breathe a prayer that these records will endure until the wind and the rain alone shall wear them away."
>
> Gutzon Borglum.

Over two million people visit the memorial each year to share this enduring vision and pay their respects to four of America's greatest of presidents and leaders.

Twenty-five miles northeast of Mt. Rushmore, on a gorgeous, winding secondary road, is Rapid City. I had never been there before, but as the second largest city in South Dakota, I expected it to be bigger than it was, 46,000 and falling. Maybe normal winter temperatures of single digits has something to do with the population shift, but this day could not have been any prettier. The fall colors were in full splendor creating a postcard view at nearly every turn in the road.

Of course, there is one place anyone on a motorcycle in the Black Hills of South Dakota cannot afford to miss no matter what time of year: Sturgis, "Rally Capital of the World." If the presidential sculptures were somewhat of a letdown because of their size, Sturgis was a total blowout on Sunday, September 26. The motorcycle museum was closed every Sunday and Monday, the summer rally had long since been cleaned up, and the police had not yet started buying more ammunition and tear gas for the next August *celebration* by biker enthusiasts. Sturgis looked just like you would expect a South Dakota farm town of 5,184 people to be if you had not heard the stories and seen the pictures of the Harley Davidson hell-raisers in full pagentry, legal and otherwise.

Thirty-five miles later we crossed into Wyoming, one of those western states that seems to go on forever even though it is *only* 365 miles east to west. We had picked up I-90 back at Rapid City because it was the only road going due west in any moderately direct manner. About 90 miles from Spearfish, South Dakota, at the state line, we arrived in Gillette, Wyoming. There were the usual signs advertising campgrounds, but I started out asking the local convenience store managers which ones were best. That didn't work very well though because most of them did not camp and only knew directions to whichever one was closest to their store. My preference was to camp somewhere near or within city limits so that I could set up my camper, leave Peppy on guard, and go for a walk to get some dinner at a restaurant. The "Crazy Woman Campground" filled the bill perfectly. It had a perfectly level grass area set aside for the "tenters" (so as to differentiate the lower class campers from those whose RV's stretched up to 40 feet and *had to have* hook ups for water, electricity, sewer, and cable TV). This was fine with me since the other tenters were among the most interesting and nature-loving people I met on the whole trip anyway. This particular night, an eight-foot canvas tent was already set up about 30 yards from our spot, but nobody was there, just the tent. After about a half hour of getting my camper ready for the night, feeding Peppy, hooking his leash up to one of the safety chains on the trailer hitch, and washing up in the community washroom, I was ready to walk into town for dinner. Just then, a jeep pulled up to the empty tent and a young couple, with sleeping bags, emerged. They were extremely interested in my motorcycle, Peppy, the trailer and rig, and the trip in general. As a result, we talked for a while, and then they invited me to have dinner with them in town. They knew the back trail out of the campground to Main Street, and I just followed them to the local Italian eatery. "Bud and Nancy" were just returning from a day's hiking up in Thunder Basin and had to go back to Casper tomorrow where she was a hospital nurse. Bud had been a geologist for some oil exploration company but had lost his job a few months earlier and was doing some independent work for several small exploration companies in Wyoming.

It warmed my heart to hear him talk about how he resented company politics, uncertainties over ownership of mineral rights, and buy-outs of properties he had worked long and hard at to make productive. I would be very surprised if he ever went back to work for another medium or large-sized company after the way he vented his frustrations that evening. For some reason, after we had a few beers, and maybe a few more beers, all our past and present employers became more and more unfair, opportunistic, and just plain ignorant. In addition, they were totally devoid of really good personnel skills, we all agreed, (which was obvious because each of us had offered them our outstanding and profitable services, which they declined!)

Bud and Nancy were wonderful company that evening. After lots of good laughs, we headed back to camp at 11 o'clock when the proprietor said it was closing time. Some states do not serve alcohol on Sunday at all, some serve only if you have a "special license," and some, like Wyoming, don't seem to have any restrictions at all. I went to bed that night feeling good - I love Wyoming and especially the rugged individualistic people who live there.

L. to R.: George, Thomas, Teddy, and Abe?

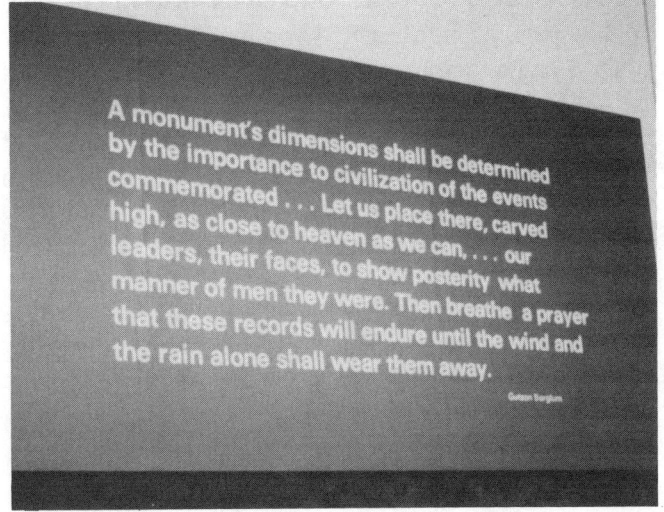

The sculptor's philosophy.

Day 3: WYOMING

For all practical purposes, there is only one way to go west from Gillette, Wyoming: I-90. In this case, however, it was not bad at all. For some reason unknown to me, this was not a big day for big trucks and the interstate was actually quite pleasant for the 75 miles to the town of Buffalo. It helped, of course, that it was another absolutely beautiful fall day with only light breezes and scattered clouds. Talk about remote, there is not even one other town on the map for 70 miles in this part of northeast Wyoming. Over and over again, I came to appreciate and respect the reliability of my big Honda GoldWing. It seemed to just purr along, as quietly efficient as any two wheeled mode of transportation could be for covering a lot of ground in one day. Many times I would secretly envy the hearty rumble that the Harley Davidson bikes made when pulling out of a gas station or restaurant, but out here, on the open road in the middle of nowhere, I was relieved and satisfied to know that my bike could go for thousands and thousands of miles with only periodic maintenance like oil and filters. My Aspencade had about 22,000 miles on the odometer when we left Parker, and the plan was to cover another 10,000 miles on this journey. The last thing I needed was a lot of mechanical breakdowns. Another "form follows function" item that I liked very much was the big, comfortable seat. Several of the fellow GoldWing chapter members Sandy and I had toured with swore by their after-market replacement seats on both the GL1200's and GL1100's, but I never had the *justifiable* urge to spend another $400 to $500 on improving a seat which I already thought was pretty darn good to my posterior anyway for long periods at a time. Regardless of the seat's comfort, however, Peppy and I were usually ready for a walk around break every hour and a half to two hours on the outside. We were not trying to break any speed records and usually met some of the trip's most interesting people at the roadside rest areas or scenic pull-offs. The rest areas, of course, were another advantage of the interstates, predictable in both distance and facilities. Since many other travelers had preceded our visit, some of whom also had canine pets, Peppy was constantly engaged in a sniff-sniff, track-em-down, where'd-they-go, routine. Often he could not stand the excitement of having so many different competing interests at one time...squirrels to chase, big trees to salute, fresh scents to follow - boy, oh boy, do we love the rest areas! Yet with all this variety of scenery and activity, Peppy was *never* missing when it was time to leave. He would seemingly time his little expeditions so that, after a quick tour of the more remote sniffs, he could see me and be within earshot of that ever-mindful command: "Let's go Pep...Hup, hup." He is a great traveler and companion if ever there was one. I loved to pull off just to see him go through his routine of "checking out" a new place. Sometimes, other pet owners would pick up their miniature dogs and run at the site of a full-grown Border Collie. Others, somewhat like myself, would look for those tell-tale signs of friend or foe, gentleman or rogue. Peppy always respected other dogs in a new surrounding, knowing that he had no more right to be there than they did and, diplomatically, always preferring to avoid a direct physical confrontation if at all possible. When not possible, however, he was no coward and has stood up to many adversaries which took more guts than brains, the way I sized up the odds. But, since I was supposed to be in control of this whole expedition, and since *any* altercations requiring visits to doctors' offices would at the very least be time-consuming and expensive, I steered Pep away from German Shepherds, Dobermans, Rotweillers, and Huskies if they even pretended to be out for blood. Cats were another matter. If they ran, and he thought I wasn't looking, he'd chase a feline as easily as a vermin. Matter of fact, I've also seen him try to round up a calf until it ran back to its 600-pound mother who showed her horns in disapproval to a wolf relative chasing her brood. Well, that's where discretion comes in and away we go.

Geographically, this section of Wyoming, the northeast quadrant, is an extension of the Great Plains forming its western boundary area, broken only by the Black Hills National Forest at the border with South Dakota. Perhaps the reason for such a sparse population in the whole state, but particularly in this section, is the dry climate, and even drier soil, with sagebrush and greasewood covering more than 40 percent of the land area. The Powder River and, about 15 miles further west, the Crazy Woman Creek, were the only surface water drainage systems for the 70 miles from Gillette to Buffalo, Wyoming. Even these two were pretty meager this time of the year. The long, hot summer had taken its toll on the surface moisture the previous months, and it was still too early for any significant snow precipitation. The key word here is "significant." It can snow in Wyoming (or Colorado) at elevations of 7000 ft. and higher *anytime* after the Fourth of July when the right atmospheric conditions exist, although there won't be any *significant* accumulations until the end of October.

Right after passing through the town of Buffalo, we turned off of the interstate and headed west on Highway 16. This route would take us over the Bighorn Mountains which are part of the Central Rockies. The change in terrain and elevations reminded me of leaving Denver heading west. The roads climb almost immediately to the switchbacks of mountain driving, slowing down speeds and increasing spectacular views. The Powder River Pass is 9,666 feet above sea level, similar to the elevation and vegetation of similar passes in Colorado, e.g., Berthoud, Rabbit Ears, and Vail, but completely in contrast to the wind-beaten and barren ones like Loveland or Independence. There are lots of Engelmann spruce, lodgepole pine, Douglas fir, and aspen in these mountains adding colors and texture to the scenic wilderness. The colors back in Buffalo were actually more spectacular since the winter cold and wind at these elevations had already turned the fall foliage past its prime.

From this vantage point, it was almost straight downhill to the thriving little town of Ten Sleep, elevation 4,206 with an official population of 311. Once again, the colors were dazzling in their brilliance from the midday sun. It was almost too hot as Peppy and I took a stroll around town, all two blocks of it including the post office. There, an official-looking plaque told the history of the town's name: the Cheyenne Indians used this route for their hunting migrations well over a hundred years ago, long before white settlers made their mining claims and the town grew up. From either the grasslands to the east or the mountain valleys to the west, it was ten days' journey to this spot on Nowood Creek, a tributary of the Big Horn River to the west.

After our stroll, Pep and I mounted up and were on our way to Worland, a town of 5,742 which seemed like a big city after Ten Sleep. Here, the dogs were tied up which isn't all bad for strangers stopping to refuel. Back in Ten Sleep there were several dogs roaming around, just free as could be, some asleep on the sidewalk, others just prowling here and there, more than a little bit curious as to who this stranger was, Peppy, that is.

From Worland, we were back on flatland heading north on Highway 16 to Greybull, paralleling the Big Horn River all the way. This is gorgeous mountain valley farm and ranch land with more cattle than sheep, but one thing is for sure, *all* the animals had thick fur coats by this time in late fall. Passing through Greybull, we turned west for Cody on the same highway, now joined by Route Nos.14, 16 and 20. It was early afternoon now and a little over 50 miles to Cody, and another 50 on the other side to reach Yellowstone by nightfall, my travel goal for the day. Fortunately, the roads in the valleys allow for a lot better time than the mountain passes do. My Aspencade has a cruise control option which makes it easier to be fairly law-abiding and still cover longer distances. I usually set my tachometer for 3100 r/p/m's which translated into 65 m/p/h on the flat and level. The carburetors automatically adjust for the thinner air at higher altitudes and I never even noticed any difference in performance between sea level and 12,000 feet.

Cody is a town similar to Buffalo, Wyoming in that they are both situated at the foot of mountains which rise up to the west. Cody, however, benefits a bunch from all the tourism. It is the eastern gateway to Yellowstone and is home to the Buffalo Bill Historical Center, a sprawling complex that includes the Whitney Gallery of Western Art and the Buffalo Bill, Plains Indian, and Winchester Museums. I stopped just long enough to walk around and realize this was a place I could spend an entire day and yet I had only an hour at this point. Peppy was not too awestruck on the historical spots; he treats all bushes and trees the same regardless of their national and state designations. If they smell interesting, he leaves his mark and on we go.

It was now about 4 o'clock in the afternoon and we still had 57 miles to the park's east entrance. I remember the time because I could not recall whether the rangers had a certain cutoff time after which new visitor passes would not be issued. So I cranked up the old GoldWing a couple of notches, and we were flying toward Yellowstone National Park. I always tried to set up camp before dark because it was so much easier to find the hooks, clamps, poles, and fittings when you can see what you're doing. I have set up the camper by the "Braille method," but it's a lot slower and, in western Wyoming, a lot colder too.

The park ranger looked like a living descendant of Buffalo Bill himself, with a bushy, full-faced gray beard hanging at least 4 to 5 inches below his chin. He wasn't concerned about the time at all, but he said the next campground in the park was another 37 miles on winding roads. His recommendation was the Pahaska

Teepee recreational area two miles back in the Shoshone National Forest. I had seen the turnoff along the way and told him I appreciated his advice. He gave me a stern warning to go with the camping suggestion, "This is Grizzly bear country. They've been doing some big encouraging for those fellas to be at home in this area. Keep an eye out, especially with the dog."

"Mister, you've got that backwards as far as I'm concerned," I said. "I expect that dog to be doing the looking out for ME!"

He laughed like Santa Claus, the first time I was sure he had a sense of humor, and waved me on through the turnaround at his gate after I paid my four dollar national park admission fee, of course.

Turning into the Pahaska Teepee Recreational Area Campground was one of the big camping surprises on my whole trip. This was September 27, exactly three weeks after Labor Day weekend, and there was not another camper in the entire place. I rode around the gravel roads and pathways a couple of times to make sure I wasn't overlooking a hidden tent somewhere next to one of the picnic tables. Nothing. Nobody. Nada. Zilch.

I had my choice of at least 20 campsites and chose the one perched next to a fast-running stream at the eastern end of the area. It was so close to the water and huge trees I felt like a great explorer, Jim Bridger himself, looking across water so cold that even Peppy jumped back when he stepped in to take a drink, pained by the freezing water's effect on his poor little paws. Then I saw it. An official sign, in official green-stenciled letters, warning "This is a Grizzly Bear Area." I wondered if the bears knew that too. Hmm, I thought, maybe this wasn't the best place to set up camp after all. Too late now. The camper was already unhooked from the bike and it was really getting dark, just about the time bears start looking around for dinner. Well, I thought, if they were going to come, I wasn't going to wait around for them since I was pretty hungry myself right now. A pristine path lead from the camp area parallel to the road for about one half mile to the Pahaska Teepee Lodge and Restaurant. I had seen it on the way in and thought it looked like a good place to have dinner. This time Peppy and I ambled our way together out of the woods, crossed the highway, and there was the restaurant. With his red collar and matching red leash to hook him up on the lodge porch deck, there was no reason for anyone to be afraid of him. On the contrary, he always managed to evoke sympathy from the passers-by who, I could see from inside the restaurant, would share their doggy bags with you know who, much to everyone's delight, especially Pep.

    Nevertheless when I came out after having a good steak myself, Peppy looked at me as if he hadn't had any nourishment since the bearground, I mean campground. So I gave him a few more filet steak scraps, dripping with the grease and gristle which he loves. Neither of us was starving on this trip, and besides, if the grizzly had to choose between Peppy and me, I wanted him to look full, *real full*. I even had an extra glass of wine with dinner just to give me a little more Dutch courage.

    Back at the camping area, nothing looked even remotely disturbed. I put on my usual night-time attire, a sweat suit, checked my .22 rifle under the storage area below the sleeping bag, and was off in dreamland before I could even imagine how scared that bear would be if he challenged two wilderness stalwarts like Peppy and me, both full of filet mignon.

Wilderness Stalwarts - Yellowstone Lake

Don't forget to take time to smell the flowers!

Ten Sleep, WY; Pop. 311 people, 4021 elk.

Day 4: YELLOWSTONE

The first thing on my mind when I woke up was not grizzly bears; it was cold! I could see my breath inside the camper and snuggled into my sleeping bag to reassure myself that the rest of my body was actually warm. I could hear Peppy stirring around outside, ready to be unhooked in order to check out anything that might have changed during the night. So I knew my next task was to muster the courage and fortitude to crawl out and face the elements while I stripped down, out of my warm sweat pants and shirt, and into cold clean clothes. This was a "natural campground" (translation: no rest rooms) so taking a normal wake-up pee meant exposing areas of myself that don't normally see daylight.

God was it cold. Frost covered the ground. Since the bike did not have a thermometer, and I did not have one in my gear, I had no idea what the actual temperature was, other than below freezing because of the frost. The stream, pure and pristine last night, was now sparkling like white jewels in the first rays of sunshine. Pep cautiously took a drink, and I might have too, if not for the warnings that parasites in mountain streams can play havoc with human intestines, and diarrhea was not high on my wish list of activities for this trip.

Yellowstone

I decided to break camp before breakfast today since we had a lot of sightseeing to do in the park, and I wanted to be ready to go as soon as possible. Fold down the tent poles and canvas, tuck the sleeping bag and cushions into their cubbyholes, strap Peppy's kennel back on top of the trailer, hook up the trailer hitch to the bike, and we were ready to go. Almost. The starter motor just clicked instead of turning over in its usual way. Should I keep trying to start the bike and take a chance on wearing down the battery, or should we walk to the lodge for breakfast and hope things had warmed up a little by the time we got back? I had never had any mechanical problems with this motorcycle, but the electrical system was supposed to be the Achilles heel of GL1200s. What would I do if I couldn't get it started? After a few more tries, however, the engine jumped to life as if nothing had happened. Eventually, I eased up on the choke, dropped the shift lever into first gear, and Peppy and I were on our way out of the "grizzly bear" campground.

A big blackboard, prominently displayed in the entryway to the Pahaska Teepee Lodge, sported the day's announcements, including the overnight low of 19 degrees Fahrenheit. No wonder the bike had trouble starting. And this was only September 28! I was later informed by the restaurant hostess that this was not unusual, and was why the park closed for the season in a few more weeks.

Maybe the cold deepened my appetite, but a "short stack" of pancakes sounded pretty good to go with the hot coffee for breakfast. When I ordered, however, I did not realize the pancakes were called "saddle blankets" because they were nine inch ovals. One completely filled me up, much less two. I would have had to miss more than dinner last night to tackle a "full stack," (three huge flapjacks with all the berries and syrup toppings you could imagine). Peppy didn't like the handouts as much as last night so we were both ready to roll, except for one stumble foot obstacle...

    The gift shop had a big sign announcing their most generous "End of the Season Sale" with all items at 30 percent off. So I bought some authentic Yellowstone souvenirs: sturdy, scenic, engraved pocket knives (made in Japan) for my two sons; gold plated earrings of miniature pine cones and aspen leaves for my daughter and wife (made in Denver); a beautiful booklet of wildlife photographs for myself (published in North Palm Beach, Florida). What is really from this area, I thought as I purchsased my souvenirs? Yes, I also bought a handful of yellow pebbles and small rocks after searching the surfaces to make sure they didn't come from Taiwan or Pakistan.

    At the east entrance to the park, the female ranger said there was no need for me to dig out my fee payment receipt from yesterday afternoon,...she remembered the distinctive rig with the dog on back. I told her about the ranger with the Santa-Claus image, and she informed me that he was her boss and the boss of all rangers. I respectfully saluted her, not the way Pep salutes a tree, and we were on our way into the granddaddy of all national parks, surrounded by spectacular scenery and wilderness options at every turn.

    I never tired of the beautiful fall days: crisp, cool air; colors that make the entire forest blush, and the excitement of a faraway adventure, on a powerful (and reliable) motorcycle with my good buddy and faithful companion behind me. This intoxicating combination made me feel like the luckiest guy in the world, free to do what I wanted more than anything else *and* having the time in which to do it. Although there have been other moments in my life when I was glad to be alive, I do not believe I fully appreciated it as much as I did right then. I was rich beyond words (and certainly beyond my meager bank account) as we rounded one exciting and panoramic curve after another.

Yellowstone inspires travelers from around the world, and I was no exception, even on this, my third visit. New Zealand and Iceland are known for their geysers, but nowhere are there as many as in Yellowstone. In fact, there are more geysers and hot springs here than in all the rest of the world put together. Why is this? At the heart of this magnificent park's past, present, and future, I learned, lies volcanism. About 2 million years ago, then 1.2 million years ago, and then again 600,000 years ago, catastrophic volcanic eruptions occurred here, according to the geologic experts. The last eruption spewed out nearly 240 cubic miles of lava-like material causing what is now the park's central portion to collapse and form a 28 by 47 mile caldera, or basin. The same magmatic heat that powered those eruptions still powers Yellowstone's famous and not so famous geysers, hot springs, fumaroles, and mud pots today. The fumaroles lack enough moisture to actually produce a water eruption like a geyser or super-heated standing water like a hot spring. Instead, they vent hot gas and acid steam, which forms a mudpot when the surrounding rock and clay decompose. They still had the prominent odor of sulfur, rotten eggs that is, when I observed them and were not as spectacular to watch as the geysers, especially Old Faithful.

The awesome Grand Canyon of the Yellowstone provided a glimpse of the earth's interior: its waterfalls highlight the boundaries of lava flows and thermal formations, interspersed with hard rock granite outcroppings forming peaks and promontories; we were 1,000 feet above the canyon bottom at our overlook. Rugged mountains flank the park's volcanic plateau, distinctly separating the core of Yellowstone from the outlying areas and, indeed, the entire world. The Yellowstone River drops over 308 feet at the Lower Falls, and over 109 feet at the Upper Falls. The rush of such huge amounts of water, churning up enormous clouds of spray and mist, was breathtaking. Hot water, acting on the volcanic rock, created the canyon's colors. Originally, I discovered, the Minnetaree Indians had a name for the river's yellow banks which French fur trappers translated as "roche jaune" (yellow stone). Although the canyon has been rapidly down cut by great glacial activity in the geologic past, scientists say that very little deepening is taking place today, in spite of what seems to be the powerful water erosion force from the river's velocity.

Although I was not fortunate enough to see everything, the wildlife in Yellowstone boggles the mind. There are a greater number and variety of wild animals in their native habitat here than anywhere else in the 48 contiguous states, and it is the only place where a wild buffalo herd has survived continuously since primitive times. Other wildlife that abound within the park include elk, grizzly and black bears, trumpeter swans, coyote, pronghorn antelope, mule deer, bighorn sheep, moose, and my favorite, ground squirrels and yellow bellied marmots (which I had earlier accused of being overgrown prairie dogs).

Yellowstone

Only a small portion of this huge park is accessible by roads. The vastness can best be appreciated by trying to cover over 1,000 miles of foot trails through the backcountry. Peppy would eagerly commit walking and running suicide by exhaustion, if I would let him, and he would die with a smile on his face as the last squirrel or rabbit eluded his jaws, outstretched in anticipation of what was never to be. More than once, when walking, I have seen Peppy, exhausted, tongue hanging out, and ready to plop down as soon as we stopped or even slowed down, suddenly spring to life when a rabbit ran across the path. You'd think Peppy had been reincarnated as a nine-month old puppy, tearing after that fluffy, furry-tailed critter who was scared to death by the onrush of a vicious canine.

About 17 miles from the east entrance, we crossed over Sylvan Pass, 8,350 feet above sea level, and part of the Absaroka Range. To the north was Avalanche Peak; to the south, Mt. Doane. Both were over 10,500 feet high. We headed downhill from there to Yellowstone Lake, which is at 7,733 feet in altitude. Just before reaching the lake itself, we turned off for a scenic view from a cliff-type overlook. Peppy and I both enjoyed the break and a chance to watch a young boy entice the chipmunks with pieces of cut up apple (which they seemed to love). The view was breathtaking - over 110 miles of shoreline, 20 miles long and 14 miles wide, with shimmering blue water 390 feet deep. In spite of all the thermal activity, the lake's temperature is quite cold even in mid-summer, about 60 degrees at its warmest! Park pamphlets advise against swimming anywhere because of the danger of hypothermia (loss of body heat effecting your senses where you actually *think* you are warmer than you are).

The scenery inspired me to try a few self-portraits with the aid of a tripod. It was pretty easy to frame the picture. Focus and aperture are set automatically on the Minolta 3Xi. I had to run to get into the shot myself before the 10 second timer went off amidst tourists' wary glances about my sanity (and I hadn't even been swimming), but I got used to those looks on this trip. (It's not really healthy for everyone to think you're sane!)

Back on the road, we headed west toward the Fishing Bridge, but pulled off to see why all the other cars had stopped. Between the road and the lake's edge, wet-looking meadows cradled a moose cow and her calf, only 50 to 75 feet away, who were grazing along Pelican Creek. With hardly a care in her manner, the moose would look over at us occasionally and then just go back to munching on whatever vegetation was growing just under the water. Every time she raised her head, water dripped off her muzzle in a most indelicate, lip-slopping way. It was the perfect setting, an ideal environment, for this huge mammal and her youngster.

During our stop, I learned that the Fishing Bridge was so named because it used to be famous for the large amount of fish people caught there. Then, in 1973, the park authorities figured out that the intense fishing activity was interfering with the trout spawning and ceded the fishing rights back to the pelicans. This high level of trout spawning also contributes to the "friendly" area for bear-feedings which is preferable to the people feeding bears or, even worse, the bears feeding on people. Ah, the wisdom of those federal officials never ceases to amaze animal and human alike.

No trip through Yellowstone would be complete without a visit to Old Faithful, the most famous geyser in the world and part of the Upper Geyser Basin in the park. This major attraction used to erupt every 65 minutes, sending its watery plume hundreds of feet into the air, according to the park's historical information, but now the regular spectacle occurs every 74 minutes. Maybe the "Old" is becoming more pronounced than the "Faithful," although there aren't many things that don't slow down after a couple of million years.

Dogs are supposed to be on a leash all the times in the park, but we both grew weary waiting for this timely wonder of nature to happen and Pep was begging to explore for a new bush to salute. So I let him loose while I set up my tripod, in order to better photograph this geyser at the most opportune moment. Then I heard it. Some other tourists were saying, "Look at that dog in the mud...Yuk,..he's licking the geyser water." Sure enough, it was Pep, ready to do what he always does in the midst of uncertain fame - lie right down (in the warm pool) and study the whole situation. Everyone laughed at his antics, much to my relief, and even the ranger looked the other way.

When Pep climbed back onto the wooden walkway, however, I had neither the time nor the inclination to issue a warning as he started to shake off all that water and stinky muck from the hot spring pool. People scattered like cats in the rain, cussing under their breaths at such rude and inconsiderate behavior in the Old Faithful viewing area. Saved by the moment, almost, the geyser finally started to spew and by the time it reached full eruption almost all had forgotten about that soggy pet with such bad manners. Whose dog is that anyway? For some reason, he was following *me* back to my motorcycle, and wagging his tail whenever I spoke. In a moment, when no one was looking, I whispered, "Quick Pep, Hup...Hup..." and away we went, having endeared ourselves to yet another group of sensitive travelers.

A few hours later and another hundred miles down the road, we left Yellowstone National Park, none too soon for those tourists and rangers at Old Faithful, I suppose. Oh well, we all need a little comic relief to break up monotonous sight seeing, hour after hour. They ought to *pay* us for providing entertainment while they waited for Old what's his name to perform.

We sped north on Montana Highway 287, through Cameron, Virginia City, and Sheridan. Twenty-five more miles and we would reach Butte, my goal for the day. My aunt in Kansas City, Missouri had always talked about growing up in Butte, Montana and I was anxious to see this mining town of yesteryear, so famous for its soft copper and hard women, or was it the other way around? I get old stories mixed up after so many years, but I remember my aunt talking about this town a lot during the two years I lived with them in high school. I especially enjoyed hearing about how cold winter was at the ranch, how many deer a hunter worth his salt killed, and how she used to gallop on horseback over the rugged mountainside in search of new precipices and wildlife. As with most stories, the images grew bigger and better with each telling at the dinner table until finally my credulity could stand it no more.

"Did *you* actually *do* all these things?", I asked her once, my eyes popping out inches from her own.

"Well, not exactly, but I *knew* cowboys and miners and ranchers who did."

If you had ever seen my Aunt Sue, all 4 feet 11 inches of her, with the softest milk- white skin ever to cover a librarian's cheek bone, and not a single muscle showing through her dainty dresses, you'd know what a sense of relief I felt not to have to struggle with that coarse, conflicting contradiction of what was real, both past and present.

Butte turned out to be a whole lot cleaner than I expected. Mining towns always conjure up an image in my mind of being really dirty, lots of grim and soot from all the crushing and grinding of rock and mineral inherent in that type of operation. The Anaconda Company, however, had long since scaled back its operations here and the biggest employer was The Montana College of Mineral Science and Technology. I would like to have seen the 19th century mansion built by the original copper baron but time did not permit it. Again, I needed to get to my campground and set up at a site before dark.

The K.O.A. in Butte sounded like the best game in town, and I could see RV activity from the interstate, always a good sign. As with restaurants, I am always suspicious when no one else thinks this is a good place to stop, but I'm there anyway. This campground combined semi-permanent residents with those like myself, just looking to spend the night. The semi-perms always had trailers with cars and kids' toys parked anywhere you could squeeze them all in. The manager confirmed there were "visitors by the month" as well as overnight guests, but convinced me that my site would be perfect for Peppy and me. She showed me just where to park my rig. Right around back of the office, in between the dumpsters and the Laundromat, was a flat piece of ground, a little patch of grass, and a picnic table. I was learning that *anywhere* a picnic table could be placed without tipping over was called a "site," especially when you were a tent camper on a motorcycle. True, the rates were always lower for me than the 38 foot RVs requiring all the hook-ups. Many times the managers would ask me what hook-ups I needed. Often they seemed surprised to hear that I not only didn't need any, there was nothing to hook up water, electricity, sewage, or cable TV to. All I hoped for was a flush toilet, hot water in the rest room, and washer and dryer coin-ops, (especially if I hadn't used laundry facilities in four or five days.) She assured me that this campground surpassed *all* my requirements and my fee was only 8 dollars. Such a deal!

It was a good night to catch up on laundry, and the campground store sold some deli items so I didn't have to ride out for dinner. Peppy was confounded by a little black terrier-type who ran circles around our camp area, yapping like he had been appointed sole protector of this space and we, of course, were trespassers. After all the wildlife in Yellowstone, I think poor Pep couldn't figure out if this was part of the squirrel-rat family or a new type of dog he had never seen before. Mercifully, someone claimed him before we turned in for the night, allowing both Pep and me to get a welcomed and peaceful rest.

A geyser, a geezer, and
a faithful companion.

Little Yellowstone critters.

Day 5: LEWIS AND CLARK TRAIL

Waking up the next day in Butte was another cold experience but not as extreme as Yellowstone...the overnight low was exactly 32 degrees according to the local campground store manager who also doubled as the weatherperson, and a very pleasant lady she was. She told me that the owner of the "little black rat," I mean toy terrier, had inquired as to whether Peppy was vicious?

"Are you kidding me?," I replied. "He exercised unbelievable restraint in the face of extraordinary temptation by a nagging, yapping critter whose origins he was not even sure of. Peppy should get an award for being the best-behaved dog in the whole trailer park."

"Well, I just wanted to hear you say that so I could tell her I spoke with you about your dog."

I took my complimentary cup of coffee back to the camper to finish getting ready to leave. I didn't have the heart to mention to Pep what that little scoundrel had told his owner about their get-together last night. I've owned other dogs in the past that would have picked up that screeching black bundle of noxious fur by the back of his neck and shook the living daylights out him. End of story. But here Pep was a gentleman about the encounter and his character and disposition get questioned. Some justice.

At least we didn't have to tolerate any more abuse from yipping as we pulled out of the K.O.A. in Butte and headed west on I-90 for a short leg. We had again crossed the Continental Divide as we entered town last night so this morning's travel was through a mountain valley setting. The name "Montana" is derived from the Spanish meaning "mountains" and, at least in the western part of the state, there is no doubt about the accuracy of its origins. Big, beautiful mountains created great bowls of valleys that cushioned our ride that morning on Montana Highway 1. In no time we had reached our first little town, Anaconda, which had a personality all its own. An old railroad car, fully restored in all its glory, serves as the local chamber of commerce and visitors' center. A park-like setting of trees and gardens, replete with autumn flowers, afforded Peppy and me a most pleasant rest area while we ate breakfast, compliments of a Hardy's across the street. I had a biscuit and coffee while Pep ate his kibbles. Friendly folks were now ready to comment on our Colorado tags and ask how far we were going. Montana is no longer a neighboring state to Colorado and it sounded far away to the locals. One boy asked if the mountains were different there than here in Montana. He had seen pictures of Pike's Peak and seemed awed when I told him we could see it from the back deck of our house. "Yes, it is different from the mountains here in that it's a little higher, without a whole range of mountains around it, and the snow is almost year round. Santa Claus often lands there in the summer just to keep his reindeer in shape." When I said that, he gave me a look of total disgust and didn't want to hear anymore from me anyway. Some nerve to think that he still believed in Santa Claus! Once again, the time had come when departure was the diplomatic choice of action for Pep and me; mainly me, howver, this time since there were no pools of water for him to plop down in and shake off all over the bystanders.

    A few more little towns like Southern Cross, Philipsburg, Maxville, New Chicago (honest), and Bearmouth put us on the outskirts of Missoula, one of the most pleasant surprises of the entire trip. Here is a college town, the home of the University of Montana, that will always conjur up images in my mind of an idyllic commune for almost any human endeavor...living, working, schooling, even riding a motorcycle. The late fall colors were bursting all over from the huge oak, maple, and aspen trees that lined the streets. The residential areas, like all college towns, were filled with young people on sidewalks going to and from classes with napsacks of books. They were celebrating the Indian Summer in shirt sleeves, and even shorts occasionally. The town was big enough to have an air of bustle to it, but it was mixed with so many vibrant people in such a glorious setting that the overall impression was one of quiet harmony, all pieces working together in perfect unison. The area's beauty demanded a lunch stop at the college Burger King, surrounded by big oak trees and picnic tables for customers. People (girl) watching was never any better than this. As usual, Pep got all the attention, he is really cute, but what he most wanted to do was check out the squirrels. There were too many people and cars this time, though, to turn him loose here. I could have spent a lot longer in Missoula just wandering around the town, but time was a jealous mistress, and we needed to begin our trek into Idaho. Little did I realize that this afternoon would be our closest brush with death on the entire journey.

Lewis and Clark Trail

Highway 12 is the modern day route from Missoula to Lewiston, Idaho, but back in 1805, I learned, it was 180 miles of the Lewis and Clark Trail, on their expedition to explore the great Northwest. A couple we knew from our local GoldWing chapter in Aurora had told me to be sure to take this route because of its scenic beauty. If they had also told me about replicating the Lewis and Clark Trail, it had slipped my mind so I was doubly delighted to find out I'd be experiencing both natural and historic signifigance on this stretch of road. Big, broad, gradual curves became tight, twisting hairpins as Route 12 wound its way into the Bitterroot National Forest. We climbed higher and higher up the mountains and as we did, I noticed the number of trucks hauling huge loads of logs, increased, all coming down the mountainside. Apparently, the Forest Service or the Department of the Interior had opened up a new area for commercial harvest because the place was as busy as an anthill. There were generally two types of trucks passing me going the other way: the first, almost new looking, with hydraulic type arms which held their cargo in place. These were invariably driven at a slow rate of speed and the drivers were in a uniform (indicating a corporate employer). The second type of logging truck, older and in worse shape, looked like the driver was in a real hurry as they came around the corners lickety split, a younger and more roughshod driver at the wheel. I was sure to give all logging trucks a wide bearth as they were huge and enormously heavy compared to us. Right after one of these maverick trucks passed us, going down the mountain, I was going through another switchback turn a little further on when I heard a loud rumble below us. I pulled off the road, looked down at the lower turns, and saw the last logging truck had broken the chains holding its logs on, and several thousand-pound tree trunks were rolling across the road like toothpicks. The driver had stopped his truck in a short distance, and was walking back up the road to survey the damage. I was so unnerved at the timing-it could have been Peppy and me under the logs. I took some deep breaths and collected my wits. It looked like there was nobody hurt and the accident was at least a mile or two down the mountain from where we were watching. After what seemed like a long time, a ranger came down the mountain in his official green government pick-up truck and asks if I saw what happened. He was holding a CB radio microphone while he talked to me. I told him that I had turned around to look *after* I heard the logs break loose but that I was sure the driver was going too fast for his load and conditions when he passed us. The ranger nodded his head in understanding and continued on his way to investigate further. Several other logging trucks passed us coming down on our ride up to Lolo Pass. The road wasn't wide enough for me to give them the bearth I wanted, but my eyes were glued to their tie-down chains and cargo. I won't live long enough to forget that close call, especially when touring any forests on a motorcycle.

  Crossing over the top of Lolo Pass brought us into Idaho from Montana; it looks like the state line runs right along the top of the Bitterroot Range. For some atmospheric reasons that are beyond me, the humidity immediately inreased, the trees were bigger, and more water flowed on the west side of the mountains, even at the same elevations. Also, there were no logging operations that I could see in this part of Idaho even though the trees were naturally more abundant in both size and quantity. I'm sure that in other parts of Idaho, logging is big business but not on this side of Lolo Pass.

A few miles further down Highway 12 was the beginning of the Lochsa Creek flowing parallel to the two lane road. This small creek flows into the Clearwater River which feeds into the Snake River which, in turn, becomes part of the Columbia. The mighty Columbia River goes all the way to the Pacific Ocean and forms the major east-to- west boundary between Oregon and Washington state. Lewis and Clark made the entire journey by river water, but Pep and I stayed on the highway which divurged from the river after Lewiston, Idaho. On the way to Lewiston, however, we saw some of the most beautiful wooded scenery of the whole trip in the Nez Pierce National Forest and Selway Bitterroot Wilderness areas. The river flow could not have been more aptly named - "Clearwater"- with its small rapids and sparkling reflections from the afternoon sun. Even though time was pressing, we stopped often to read about the huge cedar groves and mark the dates when the Lewis and Clark expedition had passed these points. True, the roadway ran next to the flowing rivers, and we took full advantage of blacktop over canoe or raft travel, but anyone could imagine the travail and suffering of such a journey in these same locations almost 200 years ago. The natural elements were still the same, and they were formidable indeed. Cold, cold water with rocks and rapids at every other turn, thick forests dense with trees and brush to maneuver around during times of portage, a constant vigil for Indians who might not take kindly to new white faces in their territory, and the ever-present struggle to press on, mile after unforgiving mile. It's no wonder there were signs talking of discouragement and despair by the men. They thought there would be a "Northwest Passage" allowing them to float out to the Pacific Ocean. Instead, this little trecherous Lochsa Creek was the first navigable water they had seen since the headwaters of the Missouri almost three months ago. Even with my modern, internal-combustion engine to power us down the highway, the signs warned of winding roads for the next 65 miles and it was late in the day. A little saddle sore from hours and hours of riding, contemplating sweetness and light in Missoula, a close call with a cowboy truck driver to scare the holy leftovers out of me, and then comes this sign saying it's another 65 miles of beautiful but demanding road ahead, I was beginning to experience my own brand of fatigue. Looking at the trip odometer, which I reset at the start of each day, we had covered 285 miles since leaving Butte that morning. That was real close to my goal of averaging 300 miles per day. I felt the need to stop and set up camp, but there were no campgrounds in sight and, being in a national forest, there were no commercial billboards telling me how far to the next restaurant or motel. Finally, however, I came upon a little gas station/general store/ hunter supplies type place called "Kamiah" (the Indian name for "long way from nowhere"). The proprietor was doing a lively business with hunters in blaze-orange coveralls who wanted to trade in one gun for another, buy some accessories and provisions, etc. All I wanted to do was pay for my gas and find out how far it was to the next campground. Well, everybody at the counter had a different idea on where the nearest camping place was. The majority opinion finally pointed me toward

Orofino, another 25 miles down the road, and about 50 miles after that to Lewiston, my last stop in Idaho.

By now the sun was setting and, of course, we were heading due west which put that late afternoon glare right in my eyes, another reason I wanted to stop! So, when I finally saw a sign with the outline of a camper on it, I couldn't wait to pull of the road to check in. There was no campground, however, only a restaurant called "The Trail." After looking around some more, in obvious total confusion, the owner of the restaurant told me that the sign I was looking at had a camper with a hose hanging out the back end. It was a camper waste station, over there next to the sewage processing plant about 1/4 mile back up the road. "Great," I said. "I'm really tired, and I thought this was a place I could break for the night and eat dinner and breakfast here, too." Apparently that was the right thing to say to a restaurant owner because he started to get real interested in where I might be able to set up camp for the night. "Well", he said, "I've got a lot next to here, nothing fancy, but you're welcome to stay there tonight if you just want a place for you and your dog to park." That sounded good to me even if he hadn't mowed the two acres all year, and the grass and weeds were over two feet high. There was a narrow path going in but no place to turn around so we stopped at the end of our own little trail for the night, before the grass went into the woods, and put up the camper by twilight. I anticipated being able to see better in the morning and could figure out how to turn around with the help of the morning sun. We were only a hundred yards off the highway, but you'd have thought we were trying to hide from civilization with all the high goundcover all around us. Crickets and field mice were Peppy's sleeping companions that night, and I was glad to have my sleeping bag a couple of feet above the ground, which I couldn't see anyway.

    The Trail Restaurant was my only choice for dinner and a bathroom so I took my toilet kit with me as I made my way to the front of the building, about 600 yards from the "camper site." As I walked in the entryway, that old suspicious feeling came over me...why aren't there more customers here at 6:30, prime dinner hour time? There was only one other booth occupied with three women huddled together, holding hands over the table top with their heads bowed. All were dressed plainly, wore no make-up, and sported white bonnets, a cross between old Amish and neo-Salvation Army. The leader, a corpulent woman who took up an entire bench, seemed to be saying a long prayer. Not a one of them looked up as the hostess guided me to the booth next to them. I told her I wanted the booth further down, which still put only one space between me and the group leader/sorcerer.

    All during dinner, I tried to concentrate on reading the four-page Idaho newspaper, but the spiritual murmurings made me uneasy as hell. I was really afraid they would size me up for the heathen that I am, come over to "lay hands on me," and go for a tabletop conversion right there! The wispering hallelujahs drifted over my shoulder along with some other discussions on "marital duties." I was torn between my natural attraction for juicy gossip and a cold, compelling fear that I should run, screaming, right out the front door before they attempted to "save" me. Discretion told me to choke down the meat loaf, look the other way, and walk briskly to the cash register as if I had other, more worldly things on my mind. The waitress took my money for the dinner as if there was nothing unusual going on and even wished me a pleasant "Good Night."

As I reached the wonderful, refreshing, spacious outdoors, I turned and saw, through the plate glass window, that they were still huddled together, probably praying for those lost souls cursed by demon rum. (I had asked for a glass of wine, but that place was as dry as Death Valley in August.)

A campsite--"Nothing fancy".

Lewis and Clark fished here!

Day 6: WASHINGTON & OREGON

For a lot of reasons-high grass, loud crickets, and fear of spooks overpowering Pep and me in the gentile darkness-I woke up several times during the night and was more than ready for daylight when the sun, in its usual constancy, rose in the east. There was no bathrooom handy, except for the restaurant's, and I was not about to go there again just to relieve myself, so Pep and I both made do in the great outdoors. I know that I had promised a trade of eating dinner and breakfast in return for a place to park the camper, but I could not face the possibility of more holy rollers to go with my ham and eggs. I actually do have a great respect for other people's religion, especially when it provides comfort and spiritual well-being, but I cannot tolerate those who, regardless of the religion, feel everyone else should hold the same tenets as they do, or there is something wrong with them. In my earlier years I was, perhaps, more tolerant and open minded. Now the rabble rousers just plain irritate me with all the "Hell, Fire, and Damnation." This is supposed to be a free country, and so I choose not to listen to the forecasts of my own demise, burning away in some purgatory for double eternities.

So there we were, knee deep in grass and weeds, heading the wrong way, into the woods, and strongly committed to getting out of the Orofino "Park n'Pray." Since the brush was so heavy, and there was no way to turn around on the path, I left the trailer unhitched and fired up the GoldWing to circle through the grass by myself. Pep always gets excited when he sees me start to leave without him and let out a chorus of yips with jumps just to make sure I didn't overlook him. He, however, was the least of my worries.

Although an 800-pound touring motorcycle is well made for cruising down the highway, it is terrible for off-road maneuvering. I had barely started my turn when the left front crash bar hit a rock over a foot high but still hidden by the grass and out of my sight. The shock jarred me off to one side of the bike. Once it gets past 45 degrees, there is no stopping the inevitable; I hit the kill switch on the way down. My beautiful Aspencade was lying on its side in two feet of weeds looking like a wounded steed. I couldn't stand the thought of having broken my bike or, maybe worse, having to wait forever in the middle of Idaho to get it repaired. With anxious mind and adrenalin-laden body, I squatted down at its side, and just like a weightlifter jerks and presses, I pulled for all I was worth. Eventually, my big blue rose up from the ground. Putting down the side stand, I then pushed the rock out of the way and crawled on my hands and knees for the rest of the circle to the path, making sure no other surprises were in store for us. Back at the bike, I could not see any obvious damage to the frame or timing belt housing, so once again, I started the engine. Ever so slowly, I "walked" the motorcycle back out to the path, dragged the trailer around to face the same direction, hooked it up, and inched our way out to the parking lot. Luckily, there was only a scratch on the crash bar so I pulled all the weeds away from the undercarriage, and we were on our way toward Lewiston.

Not too much farther down Highway 12, the Potlatch River merged with the Clearwater and we had a genuine, free-flowing river next to the roadway. Lewis and Clark must have been relieved at this point to know they were surely going to be able to reach the Pacific by navigable waterway, with possible portages of only short distances due to rapids or log jams from fallen trees. The historic markers related how difficult the overland portions of their journey were compared to the river travel, especially after the horses and mules had been traded for rafts and canoes. This section of the Clearwater River allowed no room for foot travel. The rock walls grew straight up from the water's edge, higher and higher as the river ground its way down 150 to 200 feet of canyon. The modern day roadway had been blasted with dynamite and excavated with bulldozers to achieve even the modest width required by two lanes. Looking up from my motorcycle seat, the precipice appeared to tower ominously over the tiny travelers below. One little mischief maker on top could cause a lot of grief to vehicles on the road below. Luckily for Pep and me, no juvenile delinquents were playing on the cliffs this morning, and we made good progress on the last lap to Lewiston. About 10 miles before the town limits, the flood plain widened dramatically, causing the river bottom to revert back to its old, meandering self again. Almost simultaneously with this visual gear-shifting, the odors of modern pulp wood processing wafted under my faceshield. The first time I ever smelled this kind of paper factory, about 20 years ago outside Tuscaloosa, Alabama, I was sure I had stepped in something the dog had left behind a few minutes earlier, still fresh with those organic bacteria so pungent to the senses. This time, however, there was no need to check the bottom of my boots. I had learned to recognize the distinctive byproduct of a papermill. Now it was only a matter of which turn in the road would allow a first view of the plant. Another couple of smooth radial curves, and there it stood, an enormous structure, at least two miles long, belching out smoke above the prominent sign that proclaimed its corporate ownership, "POTLATCH." Pulp wood logs floated everywhere in the river surrounding the plant, waiting their turn to be processed, and railroad cars at the other end were being loaded to haul away the output. It was a modern chemical marvel, huge in its dimensions and relentless in its efficiency. Even more than the smell, I was shocked by the stark contrast of a peaceful yet rugged wilderness area for the last 80 miles turning so rapidly into an industrial complex, busy as a beehive in mammoth proportions. "Lewiston" may have been named for Meriwether Lewis when it was founded in 1806, but there was no doubt about the patron saint in 1993; his name was POTLATCH.

The Snake River is the border between Idaho and Washington at this point of confluence; immediately after crossing the bridge, we were in Clarkston, Washington, also a lumber town albeit of more modest proportions than Lewiston. I say "lumber town" because it is obvious that all commercial activity here is related to the huge mills, the trucks and railroads that feed them, or the people who provide the services for those who work there. This is the lifeblood of the Pacific Northwest and nowhere is it more apparent than in these two towns.

As the Snake turned northward to Lower Granite Lake and the Snake River Canyon, Highway 12 continued west on a steep climb to the top of the plateau of ridges from which the canyons had been carved. There are no town names to confirm your headings and direction, only Highway 12 westbound. It would be 104 miles before we reached Walla Walla, the next municipality of any size, almost on the Oregon border. We were really just slicing off the southwest corner of this great state of Washington, and I wished I had more time to explore Seattle and the Vancouver Sound mysteries, almost 370 miles to the northwest. As it was, however, this was a mind boggling portion of our journey, not because of vast forests or raging rivers, but due to a rather mundane sort of enterprise: agriculture.

I grew up on a dairy farm in New Jersey; my father had a couple of tractors for doing those farming chores you might associate with plowing a field, mucking out a barnyard, or baling the hay. My own farm in Keswick, Virginia, 25 years later required the regular services of a sturdy International Harvester utility tractor, three-point hitch and all, for bush-hogging and fence post-hole digging. Yet nothing in my past, or even in my imagination, prepared me for the giant machines I saw here in these Washington wheat fields. There were John Deere power monsters that looked like the Jolly Green Giant himself could be inside. These "tractors" had not two, or six, or even eight, but fully *twelve* tires, all hooked up in unison, three per wheel axle, standing taller than a guard for the Harlem Globetrotters. Steel ladders with 6 or 7 rungs on the driver's side allowed the farmer an easy climb to the operator's compartment. Later, locals familiar with these machines told me they are air-conditioned, heated, often equiped with a little TV, and usually a CB radio for close communications with other workers in the same *corporation*. No small family farm here, I thought, these power monsters are hungry for diesel fuel in 200 gallon gulps, and the initial capital outlay to purchase the tractor and implements would bankrupt many a wealthy individual. (My own tractor and assorted attachments added $2500 to my farm debts in 1968, and I was told these acre penetrators were 100 times that amount.) Of course, they can plow or disc hundreds of acres in half a day, a scale of farming I had never been exposed to before. I loved watching them do their work in the wheat fields, one on a distant rolling hill, another closer in. The grooves of planted grass looked so precise they could form a jigsaw puzzle. I had seen wheat fields in Kansas, and I had seen big tractors before, but I had never seen the giants of the plow I saw today. I am surely going to look more closely the next time we cross Kansas to see if they, too, have grown into monsters when I wasn't paying attention. But no one could overlook these tractors-on-steroids once they're in front of you. I was, indeed, impressed with their size and pulling capabilities. Awesome!

    Pep and I had had breakfast back in Lewiston, but by mid- morning, we were ready for another stop, both to refuel and "defuel." A little town called "Pomery" provided the perfect setting, a gas station-cafe combination with a park right across the street where I could sip coffee while Pep checked out the squirrel scents.

    One lady ran the whole show and she crossed over to the "gas cash register" from behind the cafe lunch counter when I came in to pay for the fuel.

Smoking and talking to the old timers without a pause, "the reason she's living with em is 'cause she's got nutin else to turn to. It's not 'cause she loves em, she just needs to have sumptin... you know, sumptin is better than nutin." It sounded like way too philosophical a conversation for me to get involved, so I just paid for the gas, coffee, and muffin and followed Pep back to the park. He could care less about who was living with whom, the *really important* question was, "Would that squirrel come down the tree or not?" Sometimes I would juice him up a bit by asking "Where is he? Is he too fast for you? Are you going to *get* him?" Whenever I say those words, he starts barking and jumping out of control just to prove to me that he does have the fervent energy to go for the chase if that varmit would only show his face, or even better, a bushy tail. Somehow, however, the squirrel never seemed to share the fun of Pep's offer. "No sense of humor," I said to Pep. "Let's go," another set of words well formed in his vocabulary as we mounted up and headed for Walla Walla.

      Many state Departments of Correction post signs along the roads bordering their prisons warning motorists not to pick up hitch-hikers. This was the case in Walla Walla, home of the state penetentiary in Washington. As if those high fences rimmed with razor blades and electric charges were not enough to tell you this is not a petting zoo! I scanned the roadsides for signs of any escaped convicts lurking in the bushes or culverts. Would they really want to steal a motorcycle, I wondered, or would he just try to jump on behind me and hold a gun to my head while I nervously rode the GoldWing with wet pants? This was not a situation that I really wanted to learn more about so I down-shifted, just as I had in the Wind River National

Grasslands of South Dakota, only this time I would not be accelerating away from rogue buffalo. Fortunately, my imagination was the only thing revved up, and we crossed into Oregon without even a fly intruding on our airspace.

The first town in Oregon was Pendleton, home of the factory famous for fine woolen garments and blankets. It was warm that day, even before I started thinking about convicts ready to slit my throat, so we showed uncommon restraint relative to factory outlets, and began our wonderful association with US Route 395. This historic secondary federal highway goes from Canada to Los Angeles today. Back in the '50s, however, before the great surge of interstate highway construction around Southern California, it was a major inland north-south route through California. We would stay on it, or try to stay on it, for almost 800 miles through Oregon, around Lake Tahoe to Reno, Nevada, back into Northern California at Yosemite National Park, and finally leaving it at Lone Pine, California, the western entrance to Death Valley. Oregon alone is 290 miles from north to south and I was running out of time.

When my wife and I originally talked about this trip, I had planned to meet her, after the first week, for a rendezvous in Sante Fe, New Mexico. It seemed to be a reachable goal for a week's traveling to put me in New Mexico after touring the Northwest. However, I was now beginning to realize that in order to be in Sante Fe on Saturday, when she had time off from work, I was going to have to cover another 1,200 miles in two days, more than I had ever ridden before. True, I was not going to spend time in Yosemite like I had in Yellowstone, but it would still be a strenuous push.

Rather than camping out in the Umatilla National Forest of northern Oregon, I decided to see how far I could go today, even riding at night, and then stay in my first motel room for convenience and a hot shower all by myself. The campgrounds often had hot showers too, it's just that you shared them with whoever else wanted to bathe at the same time. Even without our friends from Walla Walla, I was always a little uneasy when someone else came in to the shower room while I was lathering up, not so much for modesty as just for my complete incapacity to respond if someone started to steal my pants, wallet and all. The thought of my own private shower gave me warm encouragement as those endless miles of northern Oregon rolled by. It was mid-afternoon when we passed through the town of John Day, and the sun had started to set at Burns, another 69 miles farther south.

There was a considerable amount of road construction all over the country at this time of year, not just because it was the end of the summer, but, more importantly, because the congress had passed another highway bill providing *all* the states with additional money for construction and road improvements. Here at Burns, Route 395 south merged with Route 20 west and for 25 miles, directly into the setting sun, forward progress was stop-and-go depending on the judgement calls of the blacktop workers funneling traffic into one lane, usually more stop than go. When I finally got to a wide spot in the road called "Riley," I accelerated away from the control of the construction workers, who appeared to be enjoying their jobs about as much as the inmates at Walla Walla. In my haste, however,I missed the turn-off for Route 395 south and proceeded west on Route 20, for one semi-arid mile after another. Pretty soon, I became worried over not seeing any more road signs. The road had just been resurfaced, and there were no shoulders to pull off onto. Instead, it dropped a couple of inches into the desert and sagebrush, not exactly where I wanted to ride.

By now, a huge tractor-trailer had pulled up behind me, and he was threatening to push (run over) me if I did not speed up. The problem, however, was that I could not see the road with the sun glaring right in my eyes, and there were no stripes or markings of any kind on the newly paved road. I stood up on the foot pegs to peer over the top of the windshield, and searched for a place to pull off ahead. I could not even see the road as I swerved toward a pickup truck on the right, thinking if he pulled off, I could too.

As the bike skidded to a rough gravel halt, the truck driver leaned on his air horn, loud enough to wake up the dead, which almost included me at that point. I thought about trying to pull out my gun and shoot toward the speeding rig, but was too exhausted to want to fight. A cowboy emerged from the parked pickup and, after offering consolation on my close call, said he was "looking for a lost horse with a rider on top." I didn't catch his humor at that moment, but he told me I was about 30 odd miles from Hampton, Oregon. This confirmed I was not even on the right road. I had come over 20 tortuous miles out of my way only to learn I was on the wrong road, and this was among the most desolate stretches of country I had seen in over 2000 miles. To make matters worse, I was almost out of gas. This was one of the low points of my trip-exhausted, lost, nearly run over, and out of fuel. I think the stranger realized I could use some help. He told me where I had missed the 395 turn-off, how to get back there, and where the gas station was in Riley. Also, he told me to beat on the side door if they had closed for the night.

    Fortunately, the mechanic was still there a half hour later. I got some gas and directions to Wagontire, the next motel on 395 South, only 28 miles away. It was completely dark now, and almost 7:30 when I reached Wagontire, population 2. This time I did have to beat on the door to rouse the manager. He didn't seem to mind, though, and told me all the motel rooms were the same price: $20.00 cash, no credit cards and no receipts. I didn't care what his relationship was with the IRS at this point. Pep and I scuttled into Room 5. He ate his dinner, I drank mine, and we both drifted off to dreamland after 556 miles, my record travel for one long day.

Wagontire, Oregon, Pop. 2.

Wagontire International Airport

Day 7: RENO

Waking up the next morning in Wagontire, Oregon, began a day of surprises. Even though I had slept well, I was still feeling tired from the night before. Pep was anxious, as always, to go outside for his morning walk and "exploration" so I let him go sniff on his own while I headed for my long-awaited, hot, private shower. Wrong! No sooner had I turned on the hot water than it started to feel less hot. By the time I jumped in, realizing by now that time was of the essence, the cold water was almost completely turned off in order to create a warm mixture. As I was finishing up my full fledged lather, there was only "hot" water on, and it was lukewarm. Rinsing the soap off took less time than normal as the water had definitely turned cold, even though the "hot" knob was all the way on and "cold" was completely off.

"Yea, we've been thinking about getting a bigger hot water tank," the motel owner, Bill, said at the breakfast counter, "but you just never know how long it will take to pay for one. Everything costs so much here." He and his wife were the chief cook and bottle washer in this compound, I learned, and she told me they figured out their own electric bill every month because the utility people came out only once a year. Bill and his wife, Olgie, had purchased the motel/gas station/lunch counter/gift shop eight years ago and have been replacing everything, one step at a time, ever since.

It was 55 miles north to Burns and 85 miles south to Lakeview, Oregon, with virtually nothing in between. This was Bill and Olgie's entire life, I realized. Throughout my trip, I would never visit a more isolated place. To each his own, however. As he was turning my eggs over on the grill, Bill let on how he enjoyed not having to put up with rules and regulations of "townfolk."
Olgie added that they get all the company they wanted from the motel guests and, every now and then, they each took a break and went to Reno while the other one minded the store. "Reno is 5 hours drive," she said, "but it's worth it if I'm lucky at the slots." It was an enjoyable breakfast, listening to them talk and seeing all the old photos and bumper stickers pasted everywhere. When I laughed at a couple of them, Olgie told me they were for sale. Almost all the signs and pictures were anti-government, anti-social, or slightly risque'. "First of all, we kill all the lawyers" said one bumper sticker. "Hard work never hurt anyone, but why take chances?" asked another. "Ex-Wife For Sale, Take Over Payments," also made me laugh, albeit painfully. I bought all three, stuck them on the end of Peppy's kennel, and got compliments all over the country, especially about the lawyer bashing. Everyone seems to hate the lawyers. Wonder why?

Outside was a public pay phone which Bill and Olgie were quite proud to have gotten installed, although it looked to me like it had seen better days. No matter, I got a dial tone and called my wife to give her a progress report and beg for a reschedule on our rendezvous date. She immediately agreed that reaching northern New Mexico by Saturday was unrealistic, and we agreed on Wednesday instead. She would get her office work done over the weekend and take Wednesday off so we could play golf and do some shopping in Raton. This was a huge relief to me since I now had the monkey off my back of trying to make fast time over a long distance in order to keep our date. Wednesday would allow me a leisurely ride through Nevada, California, Arizona, and New Mexico. (What I did not realize as we were talking, though, was that this was one of those private phone companies that charges four dollars per minute instead of the usual long-distance rate of fifty or sixty cents. I would later protest to U.S.West, the issuer of my phone Calling Card, and they arranged for me to get a credit!)

Before leaving Wagontire, Peppy and I strolled across Route 395 to an open field on the other side. There was a sign next to a wide-rutted strip of grass and gravel proclaiming "Wagontire International Airport;" a windsock made it official. Bill told me there actually were hunters and pilots who have landed there and stayed overnight at the motel. Back at the gas pump, I decided to fill up the bike since this was not a place where I wanted to be short on fuel (again). Just like the motel rooms and breakfast counter, the gas was a "cash only" purchase at $1.99 per gallon. Bill said he would have made it over two dollars, but there was no "2" on his old pumps. If you needed gas here, I realized, you were going to pay dearly for it. Nevertheless, I didn't mind the rate, I only buy three or four gallons at a time, and this whole place was like a cross-section of Western Americana that I might not experience again. Yes, Wagontire was not a place but an experience, soon to be behind me.

It was another gorgeous fall day as we made our way south on Route395 past Little Juniper

Mountain, approaching Alkali Lake. This used to be a lake with water in it, but now it was completely dry. What was once a town had apparently left with the water, although the map showed it as being bigger than Wagontire. There was no one to talk to and no place to stop for anything, however, so we pushed on, up over Hogback Summit, elevation 5,039 feet. At the summit, we stopped at the roadside park and while looking around for a drinking fountain, a highway maintenance man pulled up to service the chemical johns. He said the water had tested positive for contamination a few years ago and as a result, the highway department had turned off all the water for drinking, including the restrooms. He did not know exactly what the contaminants were, but he assured me that they knew what they were doing. He mistook my questions as to *what* was happening for *why* they were doing it, but when I said it was only *my* ignorance, everything seemed to be okay, no feathers ruffled. The place seemed too remote to be having a problem with pollution, but again, I'm not informed about ground water aquifers and such.

Our next major stop was Lakeview, Oregon, the last town before the California border. This community borders the Freemont National Forest and got its name because of its view of Goose Lake, a tremendous body of water, over 26 miles long, providing recreation and homesites for people in both states. The little burger joint reminded me of the one in Missoula, Montana, with all the healthy-looking kids (teenagers and young adults) running around. Three girls, who either owned or managed it, demonstrated an efficiency IBM would be proud of. There was an assembly-line procedure for greeting the customer, taking the order, making an add-on recommendation, assembling the foodstuff, and finally, collecting the money at time of delivery. What was interesting to me was that this place was *not* a McDonald's or Burger King; these kids had just borrowed their customer management techniques. Nothing wrong with that, of course. Why Thomas Jefferson, third President of the United States, author of the Declaration of Independence, and founder of the University of Virginia, said that he never had an *original* idea in his entire life; everything was borrowed from earlier and greater minds than his own, especially Homer and Cicero; a truly modest statement, nonetheless.

Crossing into California for the first time involved a stop at the official state inspection station. Were these armed government agents inspecting for drugs, guns, or contraband, I wondered? Nope. They just wanted to know if I was carrying any vegetables or plants that might have a few bugs on them. It is actually an "Agricultural Inspection Station," I later learned. The guns are just for a show of authoritry in case you happened to be too attached to that Screaming Arbutus, or some other potted plant. It seems hard for me to believe, in the midst of their severe budget crisis, that this expense of scarce taxpayer resources is fully justifiable both in priority and dollar amount. Then again, they didn't ask for my opinion, and I didn't feel like bringing it up to the guard/inspector. I could tell that a sense of humor was not his long suit, especially joking about the necessity of his job.

A couple of hours more riding through ranch and farm country put us outside Susanville, a beautiful northern California town of about 6,000 people. As I refueled at the truck stop/convenience store, I was reminded of my wife's comments about California Girls being blond, tall, leggy, and sort of blase' in attitude which makes them appear to be short on intellectual retention. The gal at the cash register was no different. She didn't really look at me as she rang up the sale; she was preoccupied with her hair and fingernails, while talking to the other blond colored cashier about what they were going to do that night. I couldn't stand the intrigue so I returned to Pep who was waiting for me outside, eager to get his dish of cold water on this hot day.

It was another 80 miles to Reno after Route395 turned back east from Susanville. This was a classic afternoon touring ride on a good two-lane highway. The Plumas National Forest mountain peaks were to the west, and the forever-distant desert and sagebrush was to the east. I loved touring this part of the country but it wasn't long before the crass commercialism of Nevada intruded upon the scene.

Billboards jumped out, offering unbelievable riches if only you would visit Harrah's Casino, or the Diamond This and the Cabaret That. All proposed such good odds and grand fortune to the players of chance that I wondered how the "poor" owners of Casinos could make any money at all. I would find out before too long. We stopped again for fuel and directions near the intersection of Route 395 and I-80, which has the dubious distinction of leading to Sparks, Nevada, about 10 miles away and home of the Mustang Ranch, one of Nevada's most infamous, but legal, brothels. Flyers at the Mini Mart touted "specials" for newcomers and these advertisements made the casino promotions look like Cub Scout stuff. But once again, I was "saved" by the clock since late afternoon meant it was time to set up camp, and I was not at all sure where my camp site was going to be, but I knew I didn't want to try to find it in the dark. A few more miles on the big city overpasses, with spectacular views of downtown Reno, brought us to the turnoff signs for the Four Seasons RV Park and Campground. This was another trailer park that had semi-permanent residents as well as overnighters. The female manager said there was already another "tenter" camped out in the back of the park; she would lead me there, but she wished her husband was here so he could see my rig. "He's been wanting to get one of those big motorcycles real bad, but he's got to heal up first. He's disabled right now from a Workers' Comp. Accident." I thought it interesting that she described her husband's disability based on who was paying for it rather than how it happened. I would find out more than I wanted to know the next day, but right now, I needed to get my camper set up.

"Brian" was having a beer and rustling around in the back of his new red Chevy pick-up truck when I pulled in next to him with Pep and company. He immediately came over, introduced himself with a formal, English accent, and offered me a beer while I was opening up the camper. He was originally from Vancouver, although now he said he lived in Alberta, Canada, near Lethbridge. He had worked at a huge paper mill for over 20 years and was on an extended holiday while they did some renovations on the plant. He thought it would open again on Monday, but he would not be there and didn't really care because his union seniority protected his position. Like so many union workers I've met over the years, he had an "us against them" attitude. He felt that "they" were always trying to screw the workers, and it was only because of the unions that he and the others got what they deserved. "Management never gave us a damned thing." Maybe it was true. I've never been part of a trade union in the states, much less in Canada, but I always deplored the tactics of the labor unions in creating strife with management when often the best interests of everyone were served by working *together* to try to make a profit. Brian didn't ask my labor management philosophy, however, and I didn't force it on him. We both talked about camping, being outdoors, enjoying the western United States, and, inevitably, where to go tonight for food and entertainment. He had been here for two days already and told me about the casinos with the best tables and a giant buffet for only $9.95, all you could eat! After he assured me he was not a night owl either, we got cleaned up, fed Pep and left him to guard the camp while we went into downtown Reno in Brian's truck for a night of good food and promising luck.

A month or so before leaving on this trip, I had received a letter from an attorney in Bucks County, Pennsylvania, advising me that I was the 1/36th intestate share beneficiary of my late uncle's estate. (It was the first time I could ever remember getting a letter from a lawyer with unexpected good news!) I was somewhat embarassed that I had not seen this uncle for a number of years and, truthfully, could not even remember what he looked like. Nevertheless, I figured he had probably saved up ten or twelve thousand dollars and, after the lawyer got through taking his fees off the top, would probably result in a net check to me and my brothers of a few hundred dollars apiece. Was I ever shocked to find out this bachelor uncle's estate was worth $600,690 before expenses and $493,480 *after* the lawyer and administration fees. According to the Statement of Proposed Distribution received a week before I left, my share was to be $13,700. A healthy skepticsm kept me from getting too excited about the inheritance until I called home that night from Reno and my wife said I actually had received the check, and it was in her hot little hand. I asked her to make a copy of it and bring the original to New Mexico when she came down next Wednesday so I could endorse it for deposit. By now it was beginning to seem real. I had inherited some money from an uncle I couldn't even remember, and the lawyer's letter was not a cruel hoax. Nevertheless, I had already put the "Kill All The Lawyers" sticker on Pep's kennel, and I was not about to try to peel it off. Besides, one good lawyer deed does not make up for a multitude of sins over a number of years. They were still basically parasitic scum, and most people in the country agreed with me.

    Back at the gaming tables, I lost twenty dollars before I could digest the big dinner Brian and I had gorged on. The food wasn't that great but, yes, there were big plates of everything, from salad bars to main courses and a hundred feet of desserts just to kill any long lingering hunger pangs. Oddly enough, my new-found-wealth made me more conservative than usual about gambling. I just did not want to take any chances with money that I was not willing to lose, and I had already accomplished that feat in less than half an hour. This was my first trip to Reno, but I had been to Las Vegas many times and I have always had the same strategy: only take the same amount of money I would be willing to spend on a good night's entertainment, no more. I have heard fellow office machine dealers at conventions almost brag about gambling with thousands of dollars, but to me, that was nutty as a fruitcake. This is one vice I never got hooked on and which has never appealed to me in more than a passing fancy. I have an ex-brother in law, whom I consider a good friend, who would like nothing better than to stay up all night drinking and rolling the dice, the bigger the stakes, the better. He even moved to Las Vegas once just to be near the "action," but the lure of the tables was not enough to offset the other drawbacks of living in Las Vegas, and he moved back to Alabama after only a few months.

Brian was true to his word about not being a confirmed night owl when I convinced him it was time to head back to camp at about 10:30, although he was equally willing to kill a few more drinks at the blackjack table. We compromised, and I went to look over Harrah's famous and extensive gun and auto collection while he lost only another twenty dollars.

Back at camp, Pep jumped out of his skin he was so glad to see us, but I could not see where anything had been disturbed. There was nobody else to ask about anything so we both turned in, me with plans and schemes for my inheritance, Brian with fantasies of breaking the bank at the casino, or so I thought.

Day 8: CALIFORNIA Route 395

A delightful smell of coffee brewing wafted over my sleeping bag the next morning at the campground in Reno. Brian had already started his breakfast and offered me a cup through the canvas window of my tenting. I politely declined for the moment since I normally prefer to wash up and brush my teeth first thing when I get up. There are other people, like my wife and Brian, who cannot function without a cup of coffee as soon as they wake up. My preference is to take morning tasks one step at a time. As soon as I returned from the community washroom, however, I accepted the coffee offer, and Brian continued his story of last night.

He and his wife of many years had recently separated, and her lawyer was giving him fits over what kind of settlement would be fair, etc. He had hired his own lawyer who, for some reason, would not stand up to her lawyer and wanted to give in to whatever his estranged wife wanted. Having been through a messy divorce myself eight years ago, I could empathize with poor Brian all the way. I began to realize that one reason we had hit it off so well yesterday was that he was just plain lonely for some male comraderie when I happened to come along. (Of course, it was easy for me to agree with him about lawyers and ex-wives!) About this time in the diatribe, a man rolled himself up the path in a wheelchair and Brian introduced me to Randy, the husband of the trailer park manager who wanted to look at my rig.

Randy's chest was bound in aluminum braces from his accident, when a 1200-pound steel door had fallen on him at work, crushed his ribs, and nearly killed him. He showed me the braces, told us about his physical therapy program, and said he should be able to walk in six months or so. That's when he wanted to look for either a GoldWing or a Harley. It was almost unbelievable to me that this crippled up man could ever think about riding a motorcycle, but that was his dream. A little later in the discussion, Brian asked me about getting a flat tire out on the road, and I told both of them about the onboard air compressor for inflating the airshocks or a tire. When I removed the cap from the compressor outlet on the right hand side of the fairing, Randy rose up out of his wheelchair to peer over the saddle in order to see how it worked. (This was right after he told me how incapacitated he was from the accident and why he should be on Workers Comp. a long time. Where there's a will there's a way, I guess.) Randy mentioned that he had been married only a couple of years to his current wife. Before that, he had done some time in the Ohio State Penitentiary, where he got to know some bikers "real good."

"What in the world were you in prison for?", I asked in disbelief.

"Attempted murder" he said. Randy then recounted how, in a moment of drunken fury, he had actually tried to kill a man in a bar room fight. The other man was after his woman, and he told the judge "Yes, your honor, at that time I was really wanting to kill him." That fired up Brian who began another discourse about how much trouble women in general are, but that he had stopped by Sparks on the way into Reno and "those gals were all right."

"That's because they're working women," Randy chimed in.

Just to lighten things up a bit, I then fabricated to Brian that I, too, had stopped in Sparks on the way in yesterday, and they *all* asked about him. "That Brian looks so small, they said," (he was only 5 feet 4 inches tall), "but he's really so..o..o big" and then I held my hands 2 feet apart as if to demonstrate the length of his penile organ. We all got some raw laughter on the skit, and with that bit of earthy humor, it was time again for Pep and me to hit the road. I bid my forlorn friend farewell and pleaded with Randy to stay out of trouble.

At 6,229 feet elevation, Lake Tahoe is the highest mountain lake in the country, located on the border of California and Nevada at the eastern edge of the Sierra Nevada range. I took a little detour off Route 395 to see its crystal clear waters and feel its temperature. Pep went for a little dip, of course, but this time there were no bystanders to get soaked when he shook off. A local fisherman said the water was around 60 degrees Farenheit and added "Nobody goes for a swim in water that cold unless they're part of some polar bear club." All the water skiers had on wet suits, but the sun was shinning brightly (and warmly) for sightseeing. Although the average temperature here is 24 degrees in January, the water never freezes because it is over 1600 feet deep. More than 30 mountain streams feed into Lake Tahoe, and it is easy to see why this area has become such a popular tourist attraction, year-round. Personally, I'd prefer to have a cabin on Goose Lake, straddling the Oregon border, because it is less crowded and the attraction of Nevada gambling is not a big plus for me. They are both about the same length, Goose Lake is narrower, but Tahoe must be a hundred times more famous, and hence, the crowds.

Back on Route 395, we were quickly climbing into the Sierra Nevada range and crossed Devils Gate Pass in the Sweetwater Mountains about noon. This is part of the Emigrant Basin Wilderness Area adjacent to Yosemite National Park. After another absolutely gorgeous hour of riding, we landed in the little town of Lee Vining, the eastern gateway to the park. There was a good-sized cafe doing a brisk luncheon business, even at 1:30 on Saturday afternoon. Apparently, all the people who want to escape from the San Francisco Bay area for the weekend come up here to hike and enjoy the mountain scenery, which is spectacular, especially this time of the year.

As I was hooking Pep up to a shady spot on a wrought iron rail outside the restaurant, a well-dressed man and his wife were coming out, sporting their color matched corduroy-suede outfits. (Well-dressed compared to me in my blue jeans and leathers, although no garments could have been more practical for my mode of travel.) The gentleman immediately stopped when he saw my motorcycle rig and gave me that longing look where I knew immediately that he wished he could go too. Sure enough, he had a GoldWing back in Walnut Creek and wanted to know all about my travels with Peppy. Did the dog really like to travel? Was he good under way? How did I protect him when it rained? And then, not surprisingly, he asked about our personal safety. Had anyone tried to rob me? Did I feel comfortable at night? Everytime he asked a question, his wife would nodded in the background as if to say, "yes, what about that?"

Of course, I told them there had been no real problems other than a little rough weather in Nebraska, a little too cold in Yellowstone, an impatient truck driver in Oregon, but by and large it had been the most interesting and exciting journey of my lifetime, all 49 years of it. My enthusiasm was contagious, because he looked me right in the eyes and said he wished they could do it too... someday. His job was a Controller for some major phtographic distribution company in Oakland, and he could *never* be gone for more than a weekend at a time. His wife interjected that he might retire soon, and *then* they could take a cross-country motorcycle trip. As she spoke, however, a look of remorse came over his face. He regretted having bought their big house in 1987, he said, and now, with the real estate bust in California, he couldn't get out from under the mortgage payments, even if he did retire. I offered my best wishes for their future as I went inside to have lunch. They stayed to chat with each other and Pep for at least another 10 minutes while I watched from inside. Again, so many people had reasons, *good reasons*, why they could not take the time or money for a trip like this one. Hearing them talk was discouraging at the time, but by the end of lunch, I was grateful all over again for my windswept and extended travel opportunity.

I wanted to take another detour through Yosemite National Park, but there was no North-South route for a motorcycle, just hiking trails that you could spend days on. If I took Route 120 through the park on a westerly heading, there was no easy way to get back on Route 395. And so, regretfully, we bypassed this great and scenic national park. Nevertheless, the mountain views and broad vistas were breathtaking. Deadman's Pass was 8,036 feet high, followed by Mammouth Mountain Ski Area, and then Red Slate Mountain at 13,163 feet off to the west before descending to the town of Bishop.

We refueled here and met what must be one of the most lively motorcycle gals in all of California. She and her husband were both on Honda Magnas, hers a 750cc, I believe, and his an 1100. We started to talk about bike trips when she flat out admitted there was nothing she'd rather do more. "My brothers all had motorcycles when I was growing up," she told me "and when I married him a couple of years ago, one nice spring day, I said I just couldn't take it no more and went out and bought this bike. I rode it home and said to my husband 'you got two choices: either get on the back or stay home, cause I'm out of here.'" During her story, her husband dutifully nodded his head. She continued, "So we rode that way all last year. Then, six months ago, I said to him 'You got two choices: either get your own bike, or stay home cause this is *my* machine.'" Obviously, he did not much cater to the idea of staying home because there he was, right along side of her on his own motorcycle, waiting for her signal to zoom on out of there. They took a picture of Pep and me in front of the GoldWing, and then, in a matter of seconds, they were gone, he being damned sure not to drop too far behind his fast-charging wife.

Fort Independence Indian Reservation was another rest area stop before we reached Lone Pine late in the afternoon. Lone Pine was the perfect place to stop for the night; here, we would leave Route395 and head east tomorrow for Death Valley. The Inyo County campground was as different from Reno as night and day. A big, beautiful lake bordered the park with lots of trees and an artificial beach for anyone who cared to go for a dip. Campers were on the honor system to take an envelope, pay the $7 fee, put it into the slot in the metal box, and then find your own site. We parked right next to the lake and Pep went crazy swimming and chasing squirrels before dinner. Not one official person came up to our camp and only a couple of kids made their way over later to throw a stick in the water for Pep, which he loved to retrieve. I fed him after raising the camper, hooked him up to be a good guard dog, and rode back into the village to eat and wash my clothes.

There was a super pizza place right across the street from the laundromat so I had dinner and did the clothes at the same time. Another man there had his hands full. He was trying to fix his pick-up truck while he did the family laundry and watch three children. The kids seemed to realize they had him out gunned, and they were raising a ruckus, running around the whole place, throwing empty laundry boxes at each other, and screaming loud enough to get arrested. It was a distinct pleasure to go back to the pizza place after every 20 minute wash and dry cycle. Later, he confessed that it was hard being a single parent. I agreed with him and offered to buy the kids a pizza if he thought it would help. He looked as if he wanted to accept the offer but then in the interest of caution, he declined. I told him I'd bring one back anyway, and he sheepishly agreed. I felt like a hero later as I rode back to the campground, only a mile or 2 out of town. It has been so long since I've had to care for any little ones, and since we don't have any grandchildren yet, I just don't know if I have the patience for youngsters anymore. Sleep came quickly that night as, once again, I felt so thankful to be in my position in life, as well as on this trip.

Cool Off Time in Lone Pine, California

Day 9: DEATH VALLEY

It was 130 miles from Lone Pine, California, to the other side of Death Valley. I had never been there before so I really wanted to be prepared for today's trip, especially with a Border Collie who was a lot more tolerant of cold than hot, scorching desert. I decided to buy a block of ice to go in my cooler so that I could chop off large pieces with my hatchet for Pep's water dish inside his kennel. At least that way, he would have a cool lick while we crossed 130 miles of the hottest country in the western hemisphere. Unfortunately, the Mini Mart did not sell block ice which I had wanted to buy when I refueled the GoldWing in the morning. So, with the trailer all hooked up and Pep on the back, I rode back into town for breakfast and hopefully, some advice.

The breakfast restaurant was packed full of campers and hikers from all over California, and it was my good luck to be seated at the same table with a grizzled old guy just chock full of advice. He had been hiking the John Muir Trail for the last 23 days and 219 miles, and had just climbed Mount Whitney, the highest point in the continental United States, yesterday. He and his wife owned a picture-framing shop somewhere in suburban Los Angeles, and she was supposed to meet him today for his "return to civilization," as he put it.

My first thought, on hearing his story, was that here was another guy who got the itch to take some an extended trip, like me, *and he did it*. This was the first person I had met who said "there is not a damned thing wrong with exploring the country. It builds character, self-reliance, and a sense of accomplishment... a lot more than pushing papers around a desk all day." He was actually referring to himself, a recently retired purchasing agent for the school board somewhere, but I could readily identify with his caustic remarks. We were both thrilled not to be behind a desk on this beautiful California Sunday.

My table mate had been through Death Valley several times and gave me some pointers on what to look for where, etc. Also, more immediately important, he knew where there was a coin- operated ice machine that dispensed 10 pound blocks, only a few buildings down the the street. I asked him if he had considered writing a story of his own journals on such an interesting hike as the entire John Muir Trail, and he replied that he had, "but it is too much like work to have to put everything down on paper. I don't have a need to share my experiences with everybody." A crusty old guy if I ever met one, but I enjoyed his company for breakfast and his advice to me was well-timed, both on Death Valley and the ice blocks.

Pep surely must have thought I was losing my mind when he saw me chop that big block of ice into pieces that would fit in his doggy dish. It wasn't even hot in Lone Pine, but we were still at 6,000 feet elevation, and the thin air had that crispness that only comes from the high altitudes.

We rode directly into the rising sun after we turned east on California Route 136, about 50 miles

Death Valley

from the entrance to the Death Valley National Monument where the elevation would drop to 282 feet *below* sea level. It is interesting that the highest point in the continental United States, Mt. Whitney, and the lowest point in the western hemisphere, Death Valley, are less than 90 miles apart. The temperature leaving Lone Pine that October morning was a very comfortable 62 degrees. I was glad it was still early in the day because everyone had told me the afternoon sun is the real killer. The highest temperature ever recorded in the U.S., 134 degrees Farenheit, occurred here on July 10, 1913, at 2 o'clock in the afternoon, but I was not interested in setting any new records today.

We quickly passed the China Lake Naval Weapons Center to the south and were climbing up the western slope of the Panamint Range which forms the eastern border for Death Valley. The name was given by the prospectors and gold-seekers, many of whom lost their lives trying to cross the valley during the 1849 gold rush. I could see why. In the span of a few relatively short miles, the lack of water and vegetation had become most pronounced. Even sage brush and creosote plants disappeared as we descended farther and farther down the east side toward Stove Pipe Wells, the first stop inside the national monument. The black-crusted earth was formed from lava rock over a hundred million years ago and was as inhospitable to life as any desert environ I had ever seen. Now and then, the traces of those who had not made the crossing appeared - an overturned car on a cliff-like bank, bones so bleached by the sun it was hard to tell from what sort of species they had come, and most of all, empty space as far as the eye could see. No trees, no signs, no vegetation - nothing except the gradual curves of a descent into lower and lower elevations, and long stretches of highway in the distance.

Several times during my trip, at moments like this in the middle of a wilderness of one sort or another, I began to feel a certain smugness which comes from being able to face harsh natural elements and still prevail. And yet, invariably, as soon as I would take a deep breath of pride, something would happen to pull the wind out of my sails as fast and completely as a capsize on a sailboat. Around the corner, up ahead on this isolated desert road, home of the legendary extreme heat and lack of water, comes a girl *on a bicycle* followed by her boyfriend, both just pedaling away, one fluid motion after another. Their gaunt, muscular bodies were disgustingly dry of perspiration. It was almost cruel the way those two deprived me of my hauty sense of accomplishment, right at the moment of my feeling of conquest over nature. I was so dumfounded I didn't have time to wave, but meerly gawked at passing travelers, I heading east and they in the opposite direction.

Another 20 miles of isolated road, maybe only one or two cars, and certainly no more bicycles, put us at Stove Pipe Wells, ready for a rest. I wanted to top off the tank on the bike, even though we had come only 85 or 90 miles, just for the extra margin of safety later on. When I questioned the park ranger, he said there were quite a few people who crossed the valley, or parts of it at least, on bicycles. It was becoming more popular now since the peak summer temperatures had moderated into the fall. I laughed. It was 110 degrees at 10:30 a.m. as he was telling me about "moderate temperatures." A water hose on the side of the building allowed me to soak Pep down just to try to

Death Valley

give him a little coolness for the continuing ride. His kennel was facing forward today - I wanted him to have all the air flow possible on the road, even if the air was over 100 degrees. I could tell the heat was taking its toll on him. Normally, he is full of beans when we stop at any rest area, but not here. He was breathing heavy and ready to get under way again. I double checked his water dish, added some fresh ice chunks from the large cooler, and got myself ready to ride.

All motorcycle safety bulletins advise riders to "wear protective clothing," and for most of the trip, I did just that, full leathers including chaps on my legs and a wonderfully heavy, black leather riding jacket which Sandy had bought me as an early Christmas present. Now, however, in the middle of Death Valley at 110 dgrees before mid-day, I had to shed a few layers. I kept the jeans on my legs, but a heavy tee shirt was all that felt comfortable on my chest. Similar to not having insurance, I was even more careful to ride defensively that afternoon, trying to anticipate who *might* do what to cause some accident, with almost certain "road rash" for me. I had "lost" two other bikes during my riding lifetime, both a lot smaller than a GoldWing, and I had no tolerance for a repeat of being airborne, at any speed. Those accidents were both over 20 years ago, and now I had at least developed a more cautious attitude, tempered by maturity and hardened by previous mistakes.

Right after leaving Stove Pipe Wells, we passed an elevation sign that indicated we were below sea level. Sand dunes to the north and barren desert to the south were the order of the day for this section. Notwithstanding the couple on the bicycles, it was easy to imagine pioneers on mules and ox wagons struggling across this desert at high noon. The heat was only bearable to me and Pep because we were going 60 miles an hour. The thought of walking on foot or riding an ox cart would make a gold mine pale by comparison. Then again, like most Americans, I am fortunate enough to already have a level of creature comfort rarely experienced by prospectors in the middle of the nineteenth century. Perhaps if we had little to lose, risking one's life on a journey wouldn't seem so daunting.

When we reached the Furnace Creek Visitors' Center, elevation minus 242 feet, I was dumfounded all over again. Here, in the middle of this desert, was a full-fledged resort, complete with hotel and golf course; surrounded by green grass and date palms springing from the barren wasteland. With only 1.9 inches of average rainfall per year, this is truly an oasis. The Travertine and Texas warm springs near the mouth of the canyon, I discovered, provide water here for modern day travelers just as they did for Shoshone Indians going back over a thousand years. Their source is mysterious although minerals dissolved in the water indicate that it has flowed many miles underground from Nevada foothills to the east. Despite the popular notion that Furnace Creek was named for the high heat and temperature of the desert, the name actually came from a small smelting furnace that was built near the mouth of the canyon by early gold and silver prospectors. Nonetheless, when I felt the water in the creek at the resort entrance, it seemed aptly named to me. More than warm, it was somewhat hot to the touch, probably around 95 degrees. The resort's lush grass provided stark contrast to the sand only a few hundred yards away, and there were crows so big they almost looked like vultures scavenging around the palm trees and roadways. Of couse, Pep had to go over and look up the trees for any signs of squirrels, but I swear it looked like the crows were sizing *him* up for their next meal. For all practical purposes, this is the center of Death Valley. The National Monument Headquarters, Furnace Creek Ranch, Furnace Creek Inn, and the main campgrounds are all here. Brochures say there are 1800 date palms and thousands of tamarisk trees planted here for windbreaks over 100 years ago. They all add to the remarkable impression of a desert oasis, stunning in contrast to its barren surroundings but not enough to make me want to stay.

Before we left, however, I had to take some pictures of the 20-mule-team wagons used to haul borax out of Death Valley in the late 1800s. Like the tractors of western Washington, I was overwhelmed by their size. Each team pulled two wagons and a water tank that together weighed more than 36 tons. The haul to the railroad at Mojave was a round trip of 330 miles and took 20 days. Thousands of tons of borax were mined from this area, surpassing both gold and silver in value at the time. Today, however, tourism is the main industry by far, and it is easy to see why: there is no other place like this in the United States, and maybe the world.

As we started the climb out of the valley and up into the Amargosa Range, I took a side road detour to an overlook called Dante's View. The superb panoramic views gave a real sense of the immensity of Death Valley, surrounded by mountain walls. The elevation here is 5,475 feet. Badwater, the white salt flat directly below, is 280 feet below sea level, and Telescope Peak, the highest point in the Panamint

Range on the other side, soars to 11,049 feet. We were actually looking a mile down to the valley floor and a mile up to the mountain peak, over 21 miles away. It is spectacular in its size and harshness, 550 sqare miles below sea level (and still sinking they say.)

By early afternoon we had crossed over back into Nevada and were heading north to pick up U.S. Route 95, the main road to Las Vegas, although not yet an interstate at this point in the Amargosa Valley. The roads leading to Las Vegas are almost as depressing as the city itself, with continuous advertising for gambling casinos in the middle of the desert, no less. It's a good thing for Nevada they were pioneers in the gambling industry because there is little else going for it as a state, especially in the southern half. Hot, dry, boring highway, mile after boring mile leads to Las Vegas (Spanish for "The Meadows"). I have no idea how long ago anyone actually saw a meadow around here, but it could have been Cortez by my calculations.

A GWRRA member wrote in the "Wing World" recently that she thought all the motor vehicle drivers in Las Vegas were angry, young construction workers in pick-up trucks. That is not true. Some drive old Pontiacs and Plymouths too, but they are all angry and hot, prisoners to their jobs, frustrated with the traffic, and ready to fight on a moment's notice. Drivers cussing at each other is commonplace here. The casinos isolate their visitors from the reality of the hard work, almost slave labor, required to construct buildings in this desert metropolis. It's my guess that most of the laborers are here illegally, can't speak English well, if at all, and are glad to get any job offered to them, no matter how physically demanding. When you glance into their grimy faces at the end of the day, though, it is hardly a picture of contentment or satisfaction, looking more like rebellion to me.

I tried to get through Las Vegas as quickly as possible, but when I saw signs for a state park, it sounded too good to pass up after riding for several hours in the hot sun. Several turns and a bunch of miles later, however, the signs stopped and there was no park anywhere to be seen. It *was* too good to be true; the 7-11 store manager said they had built an apartment complex next door where the park *used to be* and just hadn't gotten around to taking those signs down.

Pep and I finally found some shade on the east side of a high school buiding, enjoying a cool drink and a walk on some grass, which is very scarce in this city. Even though it was Sunday, it still seemed like rush hour at 5 o'clock and, of course, we were right in the middle of the crunch trying to go east to the Hoover Dam. Refreshed from the school yard rest, however, I pushed on and we approached the entrance at Boulder City about 3 p.m.

Hoover Dam was even bigger than I had expected from all the pictures. Of course, backing up the Colorado River to form Lake Mead is no small task and there were also massive amounts of construction going on at the dam's side barrier walls. No parking was available on or near the road crossing in front of the dam, and tourists had to take a shuttle bus from the Arizona side if they wanted to walk around. I tried to stop at the Lake Mead National Recreation area for a campsite, but they only had spaces for RVs on concrete pads, no tent facilities offered, and none allowed. So on we go, getting a little tired by now. One of the boat mechanics at the lake was taking a break as I came out of the registration office with a long face, and realizing my predicament, gave me directions to the Oasis Camp and RV Park in Oasis, Arizona, only 15 miles down the road toward Kingman. Fortunately, this was an "oasis" with a bar and restaurant only a short walk from the campsites. It was a perfect place for us to fold, and the tent to unfold, for the night.

Guarding the Rig − in the Shade!

Day 10: ARIZONA

Waking up at the Oasis RV Park reminded me of the off-color wit who said he had never been to bed with an ugly woman, but he had "sure woke up with a few." This campground looked a lot better in the dark than it did in the daylight. All the trailers which were permanent fixtures had obvious needs for repair: broken doors or windows, cracking concrete pads, weeds growing up where they weren't supposed to be, and old cars up on cinder blocks waiting for an oil change or maybe even a new engine. None of these details were apparent to me last night, but for an eight dollar camping fee, what should I expect in the middle of the northwest Arizona desert? I didn't agree to live here the rest of my life, I was just renting a space to park and sleep for one night. Pep was much less concerned with the cosmetic details, and one sniff was as good as another as far as he was concerned. He loved *every* new place we visited, just because it was new and we hadn't been there before. Anything *new* is sort of close to "Let's Go" in his scale of priorities. The bar and grill which provided me with such an adequate steak last night wasn't open for breakfast so it was time to hit the road again, bright and early this tenth day of our adventure.

Kingman, Arizona, the next town, was about 40 miles away so I would wait a little longer for breakfast, but that was okay too since it gave me a goal of covering some ground before taking a break. I always tried to break up the day's travel; neither Pep nor I enjoyed hours at a time without any chance to stretch our legs or what have you. (Pep was really good on the "what have you." Somehow, at the end of our journey across the entire United States, I think Peppy felt it was all his territory because he had marked a bush or a tree at every stop along the way. From ancient bristle cone pines in California to cactus in Arizona and maple trees in Vermont, Pep saluted them all. What he lacked in precision, he made up with quantity and perseverance. He was probably the envy of the neighborhood pooch patrol when he got home.)

Breakfast in Kingman was worth the wait. I stopped at a pancake house that prided itself on a variety of healthy, and not-so-healthy, choices. As was often the case on this trip, Pep was a lightening rod for meeting new people. A very pleasant couple who raised Border Collies and sheep on their ranch stopped to talk about herding dogs. One of their Border Collies had won a working-dog competition somewhere in Utah. I was amazed all over again at the hand signals they said their "Bandit" understood. Even when he was beyond earshot, he would respond to "Go left, go right, round em up, bring 'em in" just by motioning with their arms. They also said, after seeing lots and lots of dogs in this breed, that Pep had "classic" Border Collie markings which made me feel especially proud of my good buddy. (I didn't tell him though for fear it would go to his head. He might start demanding equal treatment or some such nonsense.)

Leaving Kingman was leaving civilization for the next 58 miles. If there were ranches in this part of Arizona they would have to be big, really big, spreads just to support any kind of grazing stock. There was very little grass or vegetation on these high desert plains and very little visible attempts at irrigation, either with windmills or ground water. The starkness added a certain unique beauty to the countryside, however, and it was another gorgeous day for touring through it.

Geographically, the area to the north of Interstate 40 is called the Coconino Plateau, an extension of the same rock formations from which the Grand Canyon was carved by the Colorado River millions of years ago. By the time we reached Flagstaff, we were back in the Kaibab National Forest, and all was beginning to have a green appearance again. The San Francisco Mountains had traces of snow on Humphrey's Peak, the highest point in Arizona at 12,633 feet elevation. The West is so interesting in its geographical extremes, often close to one another as here, desert heat one hour and snow-covered mountains the next.

We had lunch in a beautiful park-like setting, big trees and picnic tables with million dollar views, yet the place was only a sandwich shop. If I had to live in Arizona the rest of my life, I personally could be happy with a winter home in either Tuscon or Phoenix, and a summer place here in Flagstaff or close by. The elevations of 6,000 or 7,000 feet always bring cool, crisp air which I find so envigorating to the senses. Of course, "cool and crisp" in the summer turns to "cold and frozen" in the winter, which is still alright for short durations, but long winters get old after months of digging out driveways and falling down on the ice. Also, motorcycles are at a distinct disadvantage with only two wheels in relation to traction on ice. It is no fun to be skidding around on frozen roads, ready to tip over any second, as I would find out later in Kansas on the final leg home.

Now, however, we were enjoying our ride through northern Arizona and ready for a rest area not too far from Winslow. This was a picturesque spot with big pine trees for Pep to check out and inside johns with running water for me. I left him outside with orders to stay, and since there weren't many other tourists around, I thought everything would be fine for about five minutes. When I returned, Pep was right there waiting so we loaded up and started to take off. You can imagine my surprise, when pulling out of the parking lot with the GoldWing in first gear and accelerating, to look back in the rear view mirror and see a state trooper with cruiser lights flashing. I immediately slowed and rode over to the curb as he pulled up along side the motorcycle. "What seems to be the problem, officer?" I respectfully, and fearfully, asked. Had Pepper snapped at someone while I was in the restroom? Had I double-parked my trailer and motorcycle in more than one space? Was one of my wheels ready to fall off? Why did he want to pull me over? It turns out that he had just purchased a GoldWing a few months ago and, after apologizing for turning on his lights to get my attention, said that he just wanted to know about my mileage pulling a trailer, and my stator, and my climbing ability in the mountains, and other details only a GoldWing rider would care about. He was a most agreeable fellow for a police officer, and I told him so before we parted company. He was totally into his Wing, didn't have any criminals to chase down at the moment, and simply felt like talking with somebody who had covered some ground on a big bike like his. Although I never met another

GoldWinger quite that way, it was the same thing all over the country-everyone with a big Honda enjoys talking to other riders about their past experiences and future plans.

At Winslow, I was about two-thirds of the way across Arizona, a total of 330 miles. Although my average distance per day for the entire journey would end up being around 300 miles, it was relatively easy to cover much more distance out west due to the wide open highways and generally less traffic and congestion. Interstate 40 was certainly that way since all of northern Arizona is sparsely populated, and there was very little traffic this day.

I had spoken to my wife two days ago about our planned rendezvous in Raton, New Mexico tomorrow night. We were both eager to get together again after 11 days on the road. She was anxious to actually see me in the flesh and be assured that I was still healthy and in one piece. I was looking forward to sharing with her all the wonderful places and unusual people Pep and I had encountered so far. I used to think that everyone had to pretty much think, talk, and dress the same way I did, or there was something wrong with them, maybe they were a little crazy. Now I *know* that we are *all* a little bit nuts, it just comes out in different ways, and that has made all the difference. I accept others with widely varying attitudes and experiences from my own. Whenever you start thinking that everyone should be just like you, you are not only doomed to failure, even worse, you are certain to be boring; a tasteless topping on a slice of white bread. Thank goodness for the multitude of personalities and preferences which allow some of us to enjoy collecting stamps, others to play golf or tennis, go skiing or horseback riding, and even those rare few to journey to far away places on a motorcycle, all with equal dedication and commitment. Variety *is* the spice of life.

In order to meet my wife in Raton tomorrow evening, I figured I should be in Gallup, New Mexico tonight, a distance of another 120 miles. This would leave about 380 miles from Gallup to Raton the next day. I had called earlier and made reservations at a motel recommended by the Chamber of Commerce, the El Kapp, which sounded fancier than it turned out to be. Also, Sandy was going to bring down our golf clubs with her in my truck so we could play a round before going our separate ways Wednesday- she back to her job and our home in Colorado, and me to continue my wanderlust around the country. Since I could not even be making this entire trip without her support and commitment, I really wanted our reunion to be a warm and pleasant expression of my gratitude, which included being there at the same time or before she arrived. These were my thoughts that afternoon as I pushed on through Arizona, now within 50 miles of the state line.

The town of Navajo had huge signs advertising their low prices on gas and cigarettes due to a lack of federal taxes. I believe they still have to pay state taxes, but gas at 80 cents a gallon was too good to pass up even if I bought only five gallons. There was a time long ago when I also would have stocked up on cartons of cigarettes, but fotunately for my lungs, that is a vice I haven't been addicted to for years. Like a lot of Baby Boomers, I started smoking in high school, to be "one of the boys" and continued the habit on and off until I was 40. Since quitting, I definitely have put on a few extra pounds, but the health professionals say the trade off is well worth it.

In the Indian Store there were more people smoking than not. It was almost like being forced to smoke, whether you wanted to or not, with all the grey-colored air. The man behind the cash register didn't seem very happy, an older Indian who probably resented a white person paying him for anything. I felt uncomfortable being an unwelcomed outsider and quickly crossed the state line into New Mexico as the sun was setting.

The Gallup K.O.A. had signs leading right up to the campground from I-40 and it surely looked like it was doing a good business. I waited my turn behind a couple with a huge RV and hoped my fee would not be as stiff as theirs - $24.00 with all the hook ups. When the young clerk said it was $16.00 for a tent campsite, with no hookups, I told him that was the most expensive rate I had encountered in twelve states and over 3,000 miles. He said he had no control over the rates, he just worked there. "Was there anybody in authority nearby?" I asked, trying to pretend to be polite. "No, the owners have left for the evening," he said, "and they usually don't change the prices anyway from this little sheet." He had all the rates for different size campers and how many hook-ups they needed, a cashier's bible which took all responsibility away from his judgement. "Well, tell them they sure lost one customer tonight, and I'm going to write about this place in my book. The prices here are outrageous in my opinion." He was not the least bit interested in my opinion, though, and wanted to get back to watching whatever was on the miniature TV screen behind the counter before the customers interrupted his show.

So I huffed and rode on, down the main street of Gallup in search of a place to stay. Much to my surprise, there were many motel rooms advertising prices of less than $20.00 ($19.95) a night on neon signs just a couple of miles from the K.O.A. This was especially good fortune since a motel room would save me the time of setting up the camper and taking it down again in the morning, about 40 minutes all together. The bad news was that most motels do not allow pets in the room so I parked the bike and trailer off to the side and hoped the manager would not say anything as I checked in. He was an Indian in the sense of being from India as opposed to the Navajos I met earlier. They both have dark skin but sound completly different. This motel manager was much more concerned about collecting his $20.00 than anything else so there was no confrontation over Pep.

I cleaned up a little, he had his dinner, and then it was a pleasant walk up to a restaurant. I always tried to take Pep everywhere possible for two reasons: one, it was good development for his social skills to mingle with strangers in new places, without him feeling like he was on guard protecting any property, and secondly, he was an effective icebreaker for meeting interesting people. This was a restaurant where I could sit by the window and watch Pep outside, tied up to a little tree on the grass next to the sidewalk. He always greeted strangers cautiously at first if I was not present, but eventually the wagging of his tail would show his true feelings in a matter of minutes with most visitors. Since tonight was a walk and not a ride back to the motel, my dinner included a glass or two of wine to speed along the relaxation at the end of this four-hundred mile day.

Day 11: REUNION

Waking up in a cheap motel room is pretty much the same regardless of what part of the country you're in. Everything is plastic or plastic-coated: the furniture, the flooring, the drinking cups, the lamp shades, the ice bucket, the bathroom shower stall, and even the curtains. Whatever is gained in disposability and economy is lost in warmth and charm. But again, I didn't agree to live here the rest of my life. It was comfortable, convenient, and yes, cheap. It certainly didn't matter one iota to Pep who, as usual, was more interested in when I was going to be through washing up so we could go for a morning walk.

The same restaurant where we had dinner was open for breakfast, and the same people were working there at 6:30 a.m. as were there at 9:30 last night. The only person who spoke English was the cashier, who also doubled as the hostess. The waitress would just nod her head and smile, oblivious to any remark except "Gracias" when she delivered my order of bacon and eggs. I ordered by pointing to "Number 3" on the menu and then turning my finger back toward me. She would then yell back to the cashier in Spanish, who confirmed with me that I was going to get a "Number 3." I asked her to tell the cook to hold the hot sauce since it looked like everything defaulted to a level of red-hot seasoning which would make me cry while I ate, an event I could easily pass up. I have seen friends eat Mexican food with tears in their eyes, sweat on their forehead, and smoke almost coming out of their ears, as they said "Boy, this is good salsa!" It's a taste I have never acquired and probably will not live long enough to develop, i.e., pain and nourishment at the same time.

Pep and I had a pleasant walk back to the motel although it was a little overcast this morning with the threat of rain later in the day. We had already been blessed with so many beautiful days, just perfect for motorcycle touring, I had no right to complain if we got sprinkled on now and then. Besides, I had a full set of rain gear to slip on over my leathers if a storm came up. Pep's kennel was equally well-equipped. I had purchased a heavy vinyl, zip-up cover, custom fitted to his kennel before we had left Colorado, knowing that the surest way to guarantee good weather is to be prepared for the nasty stuff. On the contrary, however, if some event like a picnic or outside rally is planned with no alternative for bad weather, you can almost count on the skies to open up with a summer drenching. The weather is perverse , and at times violent, as we would find out in Oklahoma.

A quick gathering up of our stuff from the motel room, made much easier by not having the camper to contend with, feed Pep his breakfast, finish my second cup of coffee, eliminate my first cup of coffee, and we were on our way across New Mexico to meet Sandy in Raton. Three hundred and eighty miles was longer than average for a day's travel but not a marathon. It was made easier by the fact that we were on the road before eight o'clock and would be traveling the interstates virtually the entire distance today. My plan was to have lunch in Albuquerque, about 140 miles from Gallup, and then ride up I-25 to Raton, another 240 miles including a 20-mile detour for a stop in Santa Fe. It was Sandy's birthday tomorrow, and I wanted to buy her a present with a southwestern flair in one of Santa Fe's famous, or not so famous, craft shops. After living in Arizona for 19 years, she had developed a fondness for Santa Fe architecture, adobe furnishings, and Pueblo designs. Since neither of us owned a good set of steak knives when we got married 3 years ago, that would be the beginning of my gift search.

Albuquerque was the interim goal this morning, however. We were climbing almost immediately after leaving Gallup and crossed the Continental Divide for the last time at Hosta Butte Pass, elevation 8,620 feet. If there is any uninteresting place to cross the divide, I am not aware of it. Every time we zig-zagged over the backbone of the continent, I was awed all over again with the spectacular scenery and panoramic views. The Cibola National Forest and Zuni Mountains provided the backdrop for our wilderness imagination this morning. Lodgepole pine, spruce, and hemlock filled the air with that fresh scent of the woods, and fortunately, the New Mexico Department of Highways did a fastidious job of picking up litter behind the careless tourists. Every rest area was as pristine as any naturalist could ask for, and Pep and I were both grateful for the recreation. Most of my life was burdened with the stereotyped image of New Mexico as a flat and dusty state, sort of an extension of west Texas in geography and climate. Perhaps that description may hold true in the southeastern part of the state- I've never been to Roswell, Hobbs, or Clovis- but here, in the western forests and the northern mountains, New Mexico is as close to God's country as is

Colorado, my favorite state for high, awesome grandeur. Once again, I had an immense feeling of gratitude to be able to visit so many interesting and inspiring parts of the United States I had never taken the time or had the opportunity to see before. For Pep, it was a lot of new places to salute and leave his mark; for me, it was almost a new religion. I loved every minute of it and would not hesitate to recommend this adventure to any of the bored and burned out masses of nine to five workers needing a spiritual renewal.

Small towns with names like Thoreau, Bluewater, and San Rafael passed behind us as we approached Albuquerque, the largest city in New Mexico, population 480,000. Founded by the Spanish in 1706, the city was named for the Duke of Albuquerque, then viceroy of Spain. As the Santa Fe Trail achieved importance during the 1800s, more settlers arrived. An historic plaque at a city park said the U.S. Army had built a fort there in 1846. The arrival of the railroad in 1880 spurred the growth of the city even more and today, it is the center for manufacturing, mining, timber, ranching, and Federal Government operations in the state, thriving and healthy in its growth, but not polluted or overcrowded like some cities we would pass through. There was a huge truck stop-cafeteria near the highway which seemed to be a good stopping place to refuel and pick up a few personal hygiene items. As was almost a common occurrence by now, an older couple was admiring Pep and the motorcycle rig when I came out of the building. They were very interested in our trip, the travel arrangements, etc. And then, of course, they asked where I was from. When I told them Denver, thinking nobody in Albuquerque would know of Parker, the man asked me if I knew anyone in Parker, specifically a Chuck Hasstedt? Coincidentally enough, Chuck happens to be in my Rotary Club, and I consider him a good friend even though I have known him only a few months. He is an easy guy to like with a great singing voice and a good sense of humor. Martin Ahlene then formally introduced himself and his wife and said that he had been Chuck's roommate at Northwestern Dental School years ago. He also said that he used to ride a GoldWing but had an accident four years ago which left his leg permanently stiff effectively ended his riding days. His wife said they had considered the three wheeler GoldWings but finally decided to give up the sport even though they had nourished many wonderful friendships with other riders through their club. Martin then repeated those words that I had come to hear over and over again, "I always wanted to take a trip like you're doing, around the country and all, but I just never had the time." Whenever someone would express that sentiment it made me all the more pleased that I had invested the time and money to make a cross-country trip while I still had the health and stamina to fully enjoy it. With a longing in his heart, Martin bid us farewell after making me promise to give their warm regards to Chuck Hasstedt back in Parker.

Perhaps I should not have been so surprised, I later thought to myself. Albuquerque is only 450 miles on a direct route from Denver, but I had traveled almost 3,500 miles since leaving home so it seemed to me I had met a stranger half way across the country who just happened to know a friend of mine from the Rotary Club. It is indeed a small world, especially when you are a member of groups like the GoldWing Riders and Rotary.

Interstate 25 criss-crossed with I-40 in Albuquerque, and we turned north for Santa Fe on the Pan American Freeway, as it is known here. The Rio Grande was flowing parallel to the highway for several miles as we left town. Soon the gently rolling hills were interrupted by arroyos and then, semi-mountainous terrain. It was obvious we were again gaining the altitude which we had lost on descent into Albuquerque. Although the Coronado State Park was appealing as a stop after about 40 miles, I decided to push on to Santa Fe, only another 20 miles. The turn-off from the interstate was well-marked, and we rode into the oldest town in western America by early afternoon. Santa Fe was founded in 1609 by Don Pedro de Peralta as the administrative and missionary center of the large Spanish-controlled region, comprising almost a third of present-day continental United States. I could have easily enjoyed several hours in the Palace of Governors, circa 1610, and the city's oldest of several museums. After Mexican independence from Spain in 1821, Santa Fe became an important center for commerce as the western terminus of the Santa Fe Trail. During the Mexican War in 1846, the city was occupied by U.S. troops under General Stephen Kearney. In 1850, the Territory of New Mexico was organized with Santa Fe as its capital, retaining that status when New Mexico entered the Union in 1912. It was quite enlightening for a man raised in New England, where history began with the Pilgrims on Plymouth Rock in 1622, to learn this heavy dose of historical fact standing on the steps of a museum built over 10 years before the Pilgrims set sail for the New World. I checked my American history text later when I was at home and, sure enough, very little is mentioned about the New Mexico Territory and not one word on the founding of Santa Fe. (Perhaps the author's English heritage and surname, Bailey, had something to do with his perspective. I'd like to see an American history book written by Montoya or Hernandez, just for comparison.)

But time was marching on this day in Santa Fe and I had not been successful in my search for a birthday present for my wife. The steak knives were beautifully crafted, but the prices were even more dear. If I was going to pay over a hundred dollars for a gift, I wanted to be certain that Sandy really liked it and the only way to get that consent would be to wait and make the purchase with her in Raton. Also, the streets were very narrow in the old part of town allowing no room for parking. The city-sponsored parking lots were only a short walk away, but it was a hot day, and Pep was bored after being tied up for so long. Fine crafts, sterling silver, gifts to relatives- these things mattered little to my furry friend whose most relevant brush with history was "Where did that squirrel go yesterday?" The female parking lot attendant had permitted me to park in the shade next to a fence bordering the enclosed area. After paying our fee, we were on our way north to Raton.

We passed through the eastern edge of the Sangre de Cristo Mountains as we sprinted up I-25, anxious to see Sandy again after eleven days on the road. Thirty miles south of Raton, I could see Wheeler Peak, the highest point in New Mexico at 13,161 feet. It, too, had snow on top as testimony to the difference over 6,000 feet in elevation can make. It was sunny and warm in the town of Raton, elevation 6,680 feet, when we arrived around five o'clock that afternoon.

The El Kapp Motel was anything but fancy. It had a 1940s style architecture where the motel faces what used to be the main highway, now relegated to a secondary status by I-25, a few blocks to the east. Nevertheless, I could see why the Chamber of Commerce had recommended the place- it was right next door. Their symbiotic relationship was confirmed when the motel manager said that morning coffee was available "at the Chamber office next door." I had wrongly supposed over the phone that "El Kapp" was spelled "El Capp" sort of an abbreviation for the Spanish "El Capitan" or some such rich and important title. No such luck here; it was plastic, plastic, and more plastic. But, surprisingly enough, Sandy didn't even criticize my choice of accommodations when she pulled in half an hour later. She was so glad to see Pep and me, and we to see her, that a little plastic was a minor inconvenience at this family reunion.

Day 12: NEW MEXICO

Waking up together with Sandy the next morning was a comfortable feeling after being away from her for what seemed like so long. Unrushed, we lay there in bed just talking about the day ahead. She had a mandatory conference call at eight o'clock mountain time, I needed to schedule an appointment for servicing the motorcycle, we wanted to play golf this morning and go shopping in the early afternoon before we both would part and go our separate ways again. It was going to be a full day, no matter how much planning we did, so the next step was to get cleaned up and walk over to a nearby restaurant for breakfast, before the conference call came in.

Pep and I went for a walk around the back of the motel while Sandy got ready. She always seemed to have more preparations than I and, of course, Pep was born ready to go. The alley behind the motel turned out to be the border for the backyard fences of a number of small houses, each one containing a dog determined to make more noise barking than his buddy next door when Pep and I tried to quietly walk by. If there was anyone in the entire motel still sleeping before we went on this morning stroll, they had to be awake now, unless they were either stone deaf or dead. Each dog's barking seemed to stimulate the next mutt to raise the volume and intensity a notch or two, as if he alone were sounding the alarm for the first time. Even Pep could not keep his mind on business, and had to skip a couple of bushes he normally would have saluted in full form. I was embarrassed at all the commotion we had caused as I hurriedly trotted out of this protected territory and returned to the front of the motel. Even though we were in full view of the manager's office window there, it was peace and tranquillity compared to the back alley. The manager didn't seem to mind Pep staying with us in the room anyway, that's what plastic furnishings are all about.

The Honda motorcycle shop was open before we left for breakfast so I asked for a service time, and they said just to bring the bike over whenever I was ready, and that would be fine with them. The golf course was not yet open, however, so we waited until after breakfast to get a tee time. Same answer as the Honda dealer, "come over whenever you're ready, no appointment necessary." Yes, life in a small town was certainly agreeable to us this morning.

Sandy followed me over to the motorcycle shop which was only half a mile away, located on the Raton's other main street. The motel was on the east-west artery and the Honda dealer, the bank, gift shops, and other restaurants were on the north-south street. It could not have been more simply laid out for two strangers. When I left the motorcycle, I thought the mechanic was going to pull the bike around back to a service entrance to change the oil, filter, and replace the rear drive shaft grease. Not at all, he simply pushed the bike right through the front door, placed down a service mat, and started to work on it in the aisle right next to the sparkling new bikes on the showroom floor. There was no other room in back; they had been running the shop this way for quite a while, he said. I was glad to

New Mexico

be able to get my GoldWing serviced since it had been about 5,000 miles since the last oil change although I usually changed it every 3,000 miles at home. Unbelievably, the Honda operator's manual recommends oil changes every 7,000 miles which is longer than any rider I know let's his engine go. It's just too expensive to rebuild an engine and too cheap, relatively, to change the oil more regularly in hopes of extending the power plant's life.

The Raton Country Club and Municipal Golf Course was a most interesting experience even before we hit the first ball. The pro shop manager was also the cook behind the lunch counter and the mechanic who repaired the golf carts "if ours happened to break down out on the course. It's a little rough going on parts of the cart paths for the first five holes, then it smoothes out." That was the understatement of the day, and I don't mean the part about it "smoothing out." The first cart path nearly caused the cart to tip over right in its tracks. Water runoff from rains and irrigation had eroded gullies over a foot deep in the paths, already slanted from one side to the other at 30-degree angles. Then, right in the middle of the gully would be a boulder eight or ten inches high and somehow, we were supposed to drive over that! Sandy and I both voted this course the best candidate for four-wheel drive golf carts we had ever seen or heard about. The cart paths literally jarred our teeth as we pitched and bounced along the trails. We only lost golf clubs once. After that we tied them in so tight the shafts were touching each other. My full cup of coffee was history after the first hundred yards, and we both agreed that nine holes was all our stomachs could stand of this gut wrenching obstacle course. We still laugh whenever we talk about the "golf outing" at our reunion in Raton.

Three hours later, after lunch, we were ready to pick up the motorcycle which had been serviced perfectly and at a reasonable rate. While I was paying for the service ticket, Sandy was casting wishful eyes toward a red Honda Magna sitting on the showroom floor. It had the big difference of a seat three inches lower than my GoldWing which allowed her to have both feet on the ground when stopped. Many gals cannot ride the big bikes, not because of a lack of strength, but because their inseams are not high enough to be comfortable or safe when sitting still, although they might do fine under way. When we were both enrolled in the Motorcycle Safety Course last Spring, the slow speed maneuvers were hard for her because of the difficulty stopping. The instructors came up with a different bike that had a low seat, but it wasn't nearly as nice-looking as this one in the showroom. Finally, we agreed to postpone any new commitments on motorcycles for the time being, settling instead on some serious damage to my charge card for her birthday present. A Spanish-flavor gift store had three beautiful Nambe', pewter-finish candlesticks in random heights which Sandy fell in love with, and I was most happy to buy them for her.

We walked around the picturesque stores for a while longer postponing the inevitable "good-byes" until the last moment. Then, because neither of us wanted to become melodramatic, we agreed on the next phone call time and waved each other off. Sandy had an evening class at D.U. to attend, and I had hoped to be in Texas by nightfall. She took the interstate north, and I turned east on New Mexico 87. It would be another three and a half weeks before we saw each other again, but I know she felt good to have seen Pep and me on the road, and I surely was inspired for the balance of my journey.

It was a pleasant change to have the sun at my back that afternoon. The road was illuminated for better visibility which was a good thing too, for the secondary roads in this part of New Mexico were loaded with potholes and other hazards. The potholes can be a minor nuisance if they are just a few inches deep with semi-smooth rims. The real curse to a bike, however, is a pothole that drops six inches or more, enough to throw the bike in the wrong direction if you hit it at an angle or lose your grip on the handlebars as a result of the sudden shock. A pick-up truck might only have an annoying bounce when hitting the same hole, but on two wheels, with no lateral stability, it's easy to lose the motorcycle altogether.

On this trip, I have noticed that all the roads in one state do not have the same maintenance. Apparently, the more populous counties have more influence with the legislature and the Department of Highways because there were wide variations in the quality of the secondary roads within the same state. This section of New Mexico was obviously not as influential, and even its scenery was not as magnificent as the western part of the state. Its arid plains were mixed with grasslands after we crossed Sierra Grande at 8,720 feet elevation. This would be our last taste of the high mountains, and I was already starting to miss them. Another 50 miles to Clayton, the last town in New Mexico and then we passed through the Kiowa National Grasslands area at the Texas border. The roads didn't get any better in Texas but the signs sure did. "Don't Mess With Texas" was the message to deter littering. I must have seen a hundred variations of the movie title, "Best Little Whorehouse in Texas." There was "Best Little Cafe," "Best Little Town," "Best Little Used Car Dealer," "Best Little Laundromat," etc., all prideful statements with a dash of puffery. I can't remember if the Corral RV Park said they were "the Best Little RV Park" or not, but it would have fit right in with the manager's image. He wore a big, black cowboy hat, a western style shirt, and a huge silver belt buckle to hold up his jeans. I didn't see his boots, but they had to be some kind of lizard skin. He was down-home friendly though, and he gave me a level camp site which was easy to pull through and close to the community restrooms. At six dollars a night, I was as pleased as punch and ready for dinner after setting up the tent and feeding Pep.

Before I could ride out of the park, however, a man from a nearby tent site walked over to introduce himself and chat a little. He and his wife were from northern Louisiana and had been on two- week camping trip while visiting their children and grandchildren. He was a man who just loved being outdoors and had one great story after another about their visits to different national parks. Most of all though, he wanted me to know there was a *big* difference between northern Louisiana and southern Louisiana, the former being more rolling hills, covered with trees, and populated by Protestants, while the latter was swampy, lowland dominated by the Catholics. He wasn't exactly bigoted in his descriptions, but it would not have made me feel warm toward him if I had been raised as a Catholic. And how did he know I had not? Not wanting to get on that slippery slope of religious discussion, I tactfully shifted the subject to my being hungry and asked for his supper recommendations. He had those, too. He said the barbecue place just down the road was where they had eaten earlier tonight, and he recommended the baby back ribs. After trying to eat healthy foods with Sandy last night, that was all the encouragement I needed to end the serious discourse on humanity and head for the chow line. I excused myself just as he was taking another deep breath in anticipation of his version of the war between the states, but that could wait.

  I definitely think Southerners like to talk more, especially to people they don't even know, than do New Englanders for instance. It must be a cultural trait, not always unpleasant either, to hunger for good discussion on the state of the world, or how it got this way. If I had not been hungry for more basic sustenance, and if there had been a jigger of good whiskey to lubricate those channels of discourse, I might have been a more willing participant. As it was, however, I eagerly approached the Texas BBQ Extravaganza.

  Eating barbecue in Texas is as close to a statewide religion as any activity I know of. And this place was no different. There were all kinds of barbecue: beef, chicken, pork, lamb, and buffalo and in all degrees of heat: mild, medium, hot, and finally, for those who don't really ever want to talk again anyway, "Texas hot!" It used to be called "Mexican hot," but too many Hispanics wanted to file lawsuits after they couldn't eat it so they changed the name to "Texas," a generic term which covers any and all heated taste buds. I again made my plea for "mild" to the waitress, had her repeat it back to me in Texas drawl, and then jumped into the all inclusive baked potato bar while waiting for those ribs to simmer. They were not what I would call "mild," but compared to the amount of "steam" emanating from others, I didn't complain. They did have a good hickory flavor and, most importantly, I was stuffed when I ate the next to the last one.

Pep always loves this circumstance because that means he gets to offer his opinion on the rib special, which is, he never met a rib he didn't like. Even the left-over bones from the ones I had eaten weren't too bad from his point of view. Of course, he was back at the tent keeping watch, but it didn't take him two sniffs to know there was something good, real good, in that brown bag I brought him. Even though he had long since finished his own dinner, he always pretends to be starving whenever he thinks he's in for a treat. And talk about obedience! My wish is his command after he smells the brown bag. If I wait more than a few seconds to reward him with the goodies, he starts to whine and drool at the same time, a combination he knows I cannot resist. Nevertheless, there is some satisfaction going to sleep while listening to your carnivore gnaw away at "the Best Little Rib Bones in Texas."

Day 13: TEXAS

The night in Dalhart was not a peaceful one. I never was one to believe that what you eat has anything to do with what your dreams are, but, for some reason, I tossed and turned most of the night. I kept waking up and wondering if it was time to get up, but all I saw was darkness and Pep's eyes, asking the same question. Did the BBQ ribs give him a hard time sleeping too? Were his dreams as bad as mine? ... Back at my former company, the gal who had been my moody assistant in the accounting department was now my boss, and I was working for *her*. One morning, I came into the office to find she had rearranged everything, including my desk, and moved my work area into a closet next to the furnace. When I asked her if we could talk about the changes, she just turned turned her head and swishly walked away in stoney silence. I woke up in a cold sweat, thanking God that it was just a dream.

My watch said 4:30 a.m., but I was still on Mountain Standard Time from New Mexico. If I advanced it one hour to Central Standard Time, where it should be for Texas, I'm up to 5:30 and that's a good time to get up after a stressful night. It might even be daylight when I got through with my shower and brushed my teeth. It was. The sun was rising when I came out of the washroom to start closing up the tent. I had gotten pretty smooth by now at the set-up and break- camp procedure but being able to see was still preferable to doing either in the dark. I noticed that there were several more campers and RVs this morning than had been here last night when I turned in. It seems there are a lot of travelers who prefer to drive as long as they can during the day and into the night, before they are ready or willing to stop. I believe that is more common at motels but evidently, from what I saw, campers can stretch their mileage goals as well. My usual schedule on the road was to plan for a ride of 300 miles a day which allowed me to set up camp late in the afternoon, while it was still daylight, assuming we had started before 9 o'clock in the morning. One hundred and fifty miles in the morning, and the same in the afternoon, was a pace which we could keep up day after day without strain. It was a far enough distance to travel to a different town, city, or state, but not so far as to put us in a new geographical region. Of course there were some days, when for one reason or another, we had to push marathon distances to meet someone or keep a scheduled rendezvous. But that did not happen often. The most enjoyable days were just like today: an early start in the morning, good weather forecasted, a well-marked, secondary road, and no particular place we had to be by nightfall. I had planned to spend the entire day in Texas, traveling from the northwest Panhandle south and east to Wichita Falls on Texas Route 287.

Since there was no place to buy breakfast at this campground, I was going to ride to Dumas, about 40 miles away before we stopped. As always, I made Pep wait until I went in for my breakfast before I gave him his kibbles and dried beef. There is a Purina brand of dry dog food called "Moist and Meaty" which is convenient for traveling since there are no tin cans to open or save if Pep ate only half, which was his usual serving at home. However, just reaching for a cellophane package in the cooler, and crinkling the wrapper, would tip Pep off that his feeding time was imminent, and he was always ready to eat. If I fed him before I ate, though, he would concentrate more on my leaving him than if he had his own food to occupy his attention.

    Therefore, both of us had empty stomachs this morning as we were preparing to pull out of the campground. A man who had been watching us get ready to leave from several sites away comes over with a big ear to ear grin on his face. Another one of my suspicious quirks triggered an alarm. Why was this guy so smiling and why was he coming over to talk to us, with a book in his hand, when I had no idea who he was or what he wanted? He held out his huge right hand for a shake as he introduced himself, "Top of the morning to ya, I'm Jake Ingram from down near Lubbock." My natural reflex is to hold out my right hand when someone offers me theirs. It seems like the courteous response from one gentleman to another. When I did, however, Jake, didn't let go of my hand but instead clasped his left hand over both my right hand and his, having slipped his book, a Bible, under his armpit in one smooth continuous motion. I knew this was not going to be easy, but I was not in the mood for a heavy sermon this early in the morning as I sat astride my bike, ready to leave but not having fired up the engine yet. I told him that we really were just on our way out of here, and, in somewhat less than complete honesty, had a long distance we had to travel today.

In a voice loud and gravely enough to be a preacher talking to a crowd, he waved his hand in the air, "Don't mean to hold you up. No, not at all, brother. Here, just take this little piece of paper. It's got a message on it that may help you. Look at it later, when you have a minute to yourself." Seeing my opening, I seized the moment. "Thanks very much for your kind thoughts," I said as I started the engine. "That's real nice of you. I'll be sure and read it a little later. Bye now." I never looked back as the GoldWing accelerated onto the highway toward Dumas. I rode with the same intensity as if those buffalo in South Dakota were hot on my tail. I savored the strong wind in my face as we shifted in high gear at 70 miles an hour. The open road never felt better.

The main crossroads in Dumas had a Hardee's restaurant on one corner, a perfect place for breakfast biscuits and a cup of coffee. I gave Pep his dish of kibbles and sheepishly reconnoitered the grounds before going inside. Once seated, I unfolded the little piece of paper to reveal a quote from scripture about sinners being welcomed back into the fold, no matter how wretched they may have been. Just the kind of uplifting message I wanted to hear after my nightmares at the old office. Fortunately, the restaurant also made copies of the *Panhandle Press* available for their patrons. The advertisements on pick-up truck tires and baling wire appealed to me more than they ever had in the past. I was absolutely fascinated with the 4-H club awards and new financing available on farm implement purchases. But all the while I was chewing on the sausage biscuits, I kept a watchful eye on the other customers, and I sat near the door. With no more to eat, nothing left to highlight in the paper, and half a cup of coffee to go, I walked back to the rig where Pep was being petted by an old man. Thank goodness, he had a frown on his face as if he was deep in thought or something. "Just too damn cold for me, but your dog here is plum fine." I agreed with him that Pep was a natural in cold weather, sheep dog and all. The temperature was in the low forties with a light wind. Then the man just waved and walked away as I mounted the bike, after Pep jumped into his kennel (to show off, of course). Perhaps I should have been more congenial with this old guy, but after the run-in with the preacher, I was gun-shy.

The road from Dumas to Amarillo was pretty much typical Texas Panhandle. The wind was blowing across desolate plains, but not so badly that it interfered with riding the bike safely. When I first started out on this trip, I was somewhat concerned about the trailer in the wind, fearing that it might get blown around and pull me and the bike with it. Just the opposite turned out to be true: the trailer acted like a boat anchor and actually stabilized the motorcycle in the wind, on gravel, and later, on the frozen roads of western Kansas. Since the trailer was lower and wider than the motorcycle, this makes sense, especially having two parallel wheels on the ground, I just had not anticipated this advantage.

Oil rigs and wheat fields turned to grain elevators and then glass and concrete as we reached the outskirts of Amarillo, which is Spanish for "yellow", the color of the clay soil here. I kept looking for a big "welcome" sign from T. Boone Pickens, the most famous dealmaker and corporate raider from this city, but he must have been too busy figuring out his next takeover in one of the tall office buildings. I did see a reference to Mesa Petroleum, his company, somewhere along the byways, but there was no invite attached to it so Pep and I just struggled along without him.

In spite of being a manufacturing center for heavy industry, plus having zinc smelters and oil refineries, the city has a noble and clean appearance to it, especially as it rises up from the windswept plains.

Not far out of town, the earlier threat of rain became a reality. It was a light rain, but it felt heavier because of the wind quartering from the north as we headed southeast. I stopped to don my yellow rain gear, but it didn't seem wet enough to cover Pep's kennel, depriving him of any view while under way. A very small town of Memphis, Texas was having some sort of cattle auction that afternoon, and all the streets and sidewalks were packed with farmers and ranchers pulling gooseneck trailers behind their pick up trucks. My motorcycle with trailer attached could have easily fit inside one of theirs, probably intended to carry 15 or 20 head of cattle by the size of them. Since this was close to lunch time, it looked as if every restaurant was overflowing with people from the livestock auction, so we crossed the Red River a few miles later and took a food break in Childress. The rain had turned to a mist now, and by the time I was through with lunch, the rain gear was no longer necessary. You never hear folks in this part of Texas complain about the rain, however. With a low annual rainfall and dry arid climate, almost all precipitation is good for their crops and water levels.

We had ridden over 300 miles when I reached Wichita Falls, and yet I had the impression that we had only skimmed the northern border of Texas when looking on a map. This Lone Star megastate covers a region equal in size to all of New England, New York,

Pennsylvania, Ohio, and Illinois combined, almost seven and half percent of the nation's total land area, I learned. With 17 million residents, it is the third most populous state, but still it has a density much less than the nation as a whole, due to its enormous physical size. If we had the time and the inclination, the Welcome Station map said we could ride 801 miles from north to south, and 773 miles from east to west. No wonder they say it takes two days to cross Texas; it's true. Maybe the sheer size brings out the Texans' swashbuckling image but almost everyone has it, even the women.

The Red River K.O.A. was located about 12 miles north of Wichita Falls, just off the Bailey turnpike. This was fine with me since I wanted to go into Oklahoma tomorrow anyway, and this put us right on the border. Lots of military-vehicle traffic and activity from Sheppard Air Force Base added to the healthy economic appearance of this area. The K.O.A. was a beautiful setting among big pecan trees that made up an orchard in earlier years. There were plenty of shady sites on level ground not far from the main office building which also housed the Laundromat and bar-recreation room. Behind the registration desk was a lovely gal with a warm smile and pretty dark hair and eyes, named "Denise." She seemed to enjoy hearing about my trip with Pep on the bike and all so I gave her one of my souvenir photographs of us in front of Lake Dillon in Colorado. I noticed the business cards on the counter said "Rob and Denise Williams, Your Hosts at Red River Kampgrounds of America" but then the name "Rob" had been crossed out with black ink like it was a permanent change without printing up new cards. "Yea," she said, "Rob didn't make it. Running a place like this was just too much work for him. We moved here from California a few years ago, and he ended up moving back to Mama not long after that. I was determined to stay, and I do all right on my own." This gal reminded me of my wife with her spunky personality and good looks. If I had not been happily married to Sandy, Denise is the sort of lady I would have wanted to spend more time getting to know. As it was, we shared a few good laughs about ex-husbands and ex-wives, and then I left her to take care of other customers since late afternoon is always the busiest time of the day for a campground operator. Later, when commenting to her about a lavatory in the men's washroom which needed repair, she told me the lady they had bought the campground from gave her some good advice on repair people in Texas, "NEVER, NEVER, NEVER, tell a tradesman you're NOT in a hurry to get something fixed. Because if you do, your grandchildren won't live long enough to get the job done." She then confessed to having forgotten these words of wisdom when she called the plumber a month ago about the lavatory. Now the time had come for the "Urgent Call," she said. (The plumber arrived just as I was leaving the next morning, around 8 a.m.)

    Since this campground had a bar which also served pizzas and snacks, I decided to stay in camp and have a few beers while I ate and watched the local pool sharks hustle each other. Sitting at the bar, I had the distinct pleasure of meeting Debbie and Jerry Smith, a couple who worked at a local windmill factory. I listened intently as they enthusiastically shared their work operations with everyone at the bar. It seems the main product of Carter Wind Turbines, Inc. is not windmills but wind turbines, the latter being used to generate electricity instead of pumping water. Their company's products were smaller, more efficient turbines than others previously available and allowed a small utility company or other entity to purchase a wind-powered electricity generator for only $200,000. They were a lively couple that evening and gave a demonstration of other energy forms on the dance floor as well.

WANTED: 20 Good Mules!

Death Valley: No signs of life.

Day 14: OKLAHOMA

Denise came out of the manager's office with a cup of coffee when she saw me folding up the tent on the camper. My memories this morning were one heck of a lot more pleasant than they had been the night before in Dalhart, and I was well rested. Also, it was another beautiful day here with just a light mist in the air. While I was talking to Denise about where we were heading today, another man who was from Sheppard Air Force Base came over to join the conversation. John had been at the bar last night and gave Denise a hard time about not showing up so he could dance with her. She tried to give an accurate accounting of her time and other obligations, but John wouldn't buy any of it without the promise of a raincheck, which she good-naturedly gave him, adding, "only if you're alive, though." The last remark was a reference to John's military duty as a "packer," i.e. parachute packer. He said he actually did not jump himself other than two or three times a year, but was responsible for packing the chutes of the paratroopers and trainees. In addition, he was quite proud of his two "saves," a situation where his back-up parachute had opened flawlessly when someone else's primary parachute-packing had failed. Then another guy who sold ice cream franchise trucks all over Texas came up to join the party, and I knew it was that time again. Pep and I started to pull out after wishing everyone good fortune and great friendship.

We could see Oklahoma across the Red River from the campground and another state was beckoning.

The Red River was wider here than it was in the Panhandle, forming a distinct boundary for the entire southern border of Oklahoma and northern Texas. I rode only a few miles before turning due east on Highway 70, a secondary road badly in need of repair. I didn't know what condition the road was in , however, so I just kept on going because it was the only direct route across southern Oklahoma, my intended line of travel. The road surface improved quite a bit as we came into Ardmore and just on the eastern side, but then it got worse and stayed in bad shape all the way to the Arkansas line. The people almost made up for the terrible roads, however; they were always friendly and helpful, very similar to the Texans I had met.

I was looking for a tank bag for my GL1200 GoldWing, something I thought I could buy at any Honda dealer. When you are on the road all day, as I was, it is very helpful to have the map directly in front without having to stop and open up the trunk or saddlebag to see where you are. Especially when there are a lot of small towns along the way, it is convenient for planning lunch stops, rest areas, and campgrounds. Sometimes, alternate routes are necessary due to construction, detours, or side trips. I decided I really needed one of these tank bags after getting lost a couple of times, but now that I was willing to buy one, I couldn't find a Honda dealer who had one in stock. The dealer in Durant, Oklahoma was happy to order one, but it would take four days to get it in. A Citgo gas station next door was a timely place to refuel on a credit card and the owner even allowed me to sit at his desk while I made some phone calls. He then sat on my motorcycle just to "get a feel for a big rig," which seemed like a fair trade of seats to me. One of my former accounting department assistants, whom I liked very much both as a worker and a person, had called Sandy at our home and said she needed to talk to me. Some questions had arisen about how I had handled a particularly complicated Accounts Receivable collection problem several months ago, and she did not have the complete information. When I got "Peni" on the phone she was surprised I was able to call back since Sandy had said I was out of state. I confirmed that I was in Oklahoma, but since she did not call for frivolous reasons, it seemed worth the extra effort to get back in touch. "When Peni calls, I know I'm supposed to jump through the hoops," I said. She laughed, as always, indicating an abundant sense of humor which made her such a pleasure to work with.

By the time I got to Hugo, about another 55 miles, I also realized I had run really low on cash and wanted to make an ATM withdrawal. Much to my surprise, however, the banks in Hugo did not have Automatic Teller Machines and a banker told me there were not any for a hundred miles from the Oklahoma-Arkansas state line. I never could figure out why they were all over the rest of country but not in this area. I could have gotten an advance on my Visa card, but I was too cheap to pay the extra cash advance fee. In fact, I still had my monthly payment check in the envelope to mail, along with some other checks, at the next post office, in Valiant, Oklahoma. This little town was the occasion of one of the warmest receptions Pep and I received on the entire trip, maybe because it was off the beaten path. Coming out of the post office, four ladies were admiring Pep who was just sitting on the lawn, minding his own business like a good boy while he waited for me. As always, he started to jump with excitement when I walked through the exit door much to the delight of the ladies, who thought he might have been lost. When they then saw the motorcycle rig, and watched Pep jump into it, and noticed where we were from, they could not stop the gushing and sighing. One woman hustled into a nearby farm store to get her husband who had the camera so she could take our picture. I then gave another lady a copy of the Lake Dillon travel pose much to the delight of all. As we pulled out of the parking lot, they were all waving goodbye while shouting Peppy's name. I felt almost like a hero or something to receive so much attention, although I must confess the husbands were not that impressed and thought the women were over doing it. Bah humbug on them. I liked the old gals of Valiant, Oklahoma.

The ladies' hearts were warm, but the weather had turned cold and the skies were beginning to look ominous. The banker was right. Next town of Idabel still had no cash machines, but there was the Ouachita National Forest and Broken Bow Lake Wilderness area which I was sure would have a campground. I could write a check or use a credit card to pay for the campsite and get some cash the next day. The plan was fine except we almost didn't make it to the next day.

The Beavers Bend State Campground within the wilderness area had a tent-camping site right on the Mountain Fork of the Little River, a tributary of the Red River. When I checked in late that afternoon at the main lodge, they said the policy was not to make reservations or take prepayments, just go pick out your campsite and a park ranger would be around later to collect the fee. The skies had gotten considerably darker now, and it was no longer a question of whether it would rain, but rather when and for how long. I chose a site overlooking the river, which was peaceful but full as the sun went down that afternoon. The water had a dark green color to it indicating an abundance of organic matter which had been dissolved or eroded into the river channel flowing past us. It was somewhat more difficult than usual setting up the camper since the ground was clay and rock mixed together to form a hard, rough surface. I had to pound the stakes with my hatchet to get them to stay in. They supported the guide lines for the tenting, which I was sure I would need if the wind picked up any more. The sky was impending evil; dark clouds with billowing curves were blowing past the moon with astounding speed. This was no ordinary night. The river had also picked up speed when Pep and I turned in for the evening. I had covered his kennel with the waterproof vinyl shell and tied the ends of the GoldWing tarp over the bike and under its middle. The ranger drove up in his official green pick-up truck, gave me a receipt for my fee, and confirmed that they were expecting a bad storm tonight.

    Then it began. Loud claps of thunder shattered the air with their proximity and magnitude. For the first time in my life, I could actually hear the sizzle of the heat from the lightening on the wet trees and leaves. Pep was tied up to his leash attached to the trailer safety chain so I knew he could not run off anywhere even though he would like to. If I let him into the tent with me, I knew he would shake off inside making everything wet and muddy, and he would still be scared to death with the thunder exploding around us.

Then I saw real trouble. Through the heavy torrents of rain, I was peering out the tent flap to see the GoldWing starting to list over to one side. It looked as though the rain had softened the ground under the side stand so much that the bike was going to slowly tip over from its own weight, plus all the wind blowing at near hurricane gusts. I decided I had to get soaked, if necessary, to keep the motorcycle upright. If it tipped over, the gas would leak out and all the rain water would flow into the engine cowlings and soak my lambskin seat cover too. I had the hatchet in the tent which I could slide under the kick stand to give it a wider base and more stability in the rain and mud. After a slight hesitation, hoping for a respite where there was none, I jumped out into as huge a deluge of water as I have ever felt from natural sources. It reminded me of being sprayed with the hose by one of my brothers as a kid, with the water spray adjusted all the way over to a heavy, thick flow, not a light spray at all. I struggled with the 800 pounds of motorcycle and semi-canvas cover as I wedged the head of the hand ax under the base of the stand. As I worked, my own feet were sinking into the mud, nearly up to my ankles without any boots, as I was sure they would have gotten soaked too. I could hardly see what I was doing as I tried to wipe my eyes again and again. Pep was all the way in his kennel, but it looked like the water had risen over the little transom and was going inside his bed too. I grabbed a couple of limbs which had fallen off the huge oak trees nearby and pushed them under the front, and then the back, to try to raise his kennel bottom off the soggy ground at least a few inches. It raised the kennel but was not very stable-as I could feel Pep moving around inside. I tried to tell him he was a "good boy" as another humongous thunder clap went off in the sky above us. Soaking wet and physically exhausted, I crawled back through the opening in the tent to my sleeping bag. I was genuinely afraid as I took off my wet clothes and pulled on my sweat pants and shirt, letting them serve as both towels and warmth. The GoldWing stood proud through the night as I checked on it every half hour. The water was no closer to Pep's kennel so I knew he would probably be all right even if he was scared to death now, so was I for that matter. This violent thunderstorm continued on and on throughout the night. I never dozed off for more than a few minutes at a time before the noise of thunder woke me up. It was almost as if we were under enemy fire, plus the constant water bombardments.

  Mercifully, morning and an end to the rain and thunder came at almost the same time. Opening the tent flap, I could see the ground was pock-marked with little holes from the pounding water. The campground looked more like a war zone than a recreational facility. Tree limbs littered the ground along with overturned trash cans and all the debris from inside them. The little river, calm but full last night, was raging in billowing waves as it carried brown dirt everywhere within its banks, only inches from overflowing. Lumber and other construction materials were bobbing up and down in the torrents, jerked away from wherever the construction site had been upstream. The swollen river was out of control and ready to confiscate anything in its path. It was a scene from "Deliverance" if ever there was one. I didn't care about the raging water or the damage to the park. I just wanted to get out of here. Could the motorcycle climb out of the mud- slick campground? The roads were in terrible shape from all the runoff and all surfaces were as slippery as an eel skin. Before we left, I tried to wring out all Pep's pads and his lambskin bed. After I got the damp tent all folded down, I would hang the wet pads and towels off the end of the trailer to let them blow dry in the wind while we were under way. In spite of the worst thunderstorm I had ever experienced, however, the camper tent had stayed dry inside. It was so well designed that the runoff went over the edges instead of inside the tent. The tenting fabric, while soaking wet on the outside, had still kept the water from penetrating, and I was truly grateful that Larry and his family had not gone out to the lowest bidder for materials when designing and building this rig. It was well-made and had withstood a beating from the storm of the century. We skidded our way up the park's gravel-mud trails and bid farewell to Broken Bow, Oklahoma, a place I would never forget as long as I lived. If I never saw it again, that was okay, too. Pep shared my sympathies, I'm sure. We're out of here, happy to be alive in the wet morning after a vengeful and turbulent night.

Day 15: ARKANSAS

Never did the sunshine look as good to me as it did that October morning when we crossed over the state line into Arkansas, "Home of President Bill Clinton." Notwithstanding a state's pride at having fathered a president, I was much more pleased just to be getting away from Broken Bow, Oklahoma, and those near-death storms. The lightning scared me enough, however, to do a little research: almost 200 people are killed and several hundred more are injured by lightning every year in the United States alone. This is a death rate greater than that of hurricanes and tornadoes combined, a little-known fact which I was happy not to contribute to statistically. The shock waves which I felt last night came from my proximity to the "explosion" which occurs when negative forces from the clouds make positive contact with the ground. The lightning "flashes" are the illumination of those opposite electrical charges causing an intense heating and expansion of the air which we hear as thunder. I cannot imagine any scientist, no matter how erudite and committed he might be to his research, becoming so familiar with this phenomena that he was no longer afraid when the actual clap takes place close by. It's just a magnitude of force and noise which can only be approximated by the battlefield of war itself, another situation I have no desire to participate in. However, just like those men I have known who came back from

Vietnam in one piece, I, too, was glad to be able to live through this experience, in retrospect, without any bodily damage. Close calls don't count in life's long ledger.

Several days ago, when contemplating my southern route, I had hoped to go to Hot Springs National Park and camp out in the Caddo Mountains. Now, however, since it was still early morning and I had not yet even dried out fully from last night's drenching, it was not working out time and distance wise to think about camping only 80 miles away. Also, it was possible to go through Delight, Arkansas on the way to Hot Springs. Why would anyone want to detour to include Delight, population 431? It happens to be the birthplace and boyhood home of Glenn Campbell, a singer whose country ballads had provided many hours of listening enjoyment during my western travels. Would there be streets named after him? What about a big welcome sign with his smiling picture at the town limits? No, I would just have to wait until another time to find out. I still had not gotten any cash yet, and by now I was down to my last few folding bills. Two dollars is not much when coffee and snacks are a regular part of one's daily regimen. If I turned south, I could stop at Ashdown, Arkansas, to see if the banks there had ATMs and if not, Texarkana surely could be my cash replenishment stop. A southerly route through Arkansas to Louisiana was the wisest choice, I decided, balancing all the factors involved. Glenn probably wasn't home anyway.

Ashdown had a big brick, confidence-inspiring bank on the outskirts of town, right off the main highway. It was Saturday, however, which meant the banks here were not open at all, not even limited hours, but, eureka! The MAX 24 ATM proclaimed that money was available 24 hours a day, every day of the year. When I put my bank card in the slot, and then entered my personal identification number, the computer went through its usual clicking and whirring only to respond with the message, "This is an unauthorized usage. Your last transaction has been canceled. Contact your bank immediately." I could hardly believe this response. My last transaction had been Sandy's deposit of my inheritance check when she went back home after we met in New Mexico. Could it be that the inheritance check from the lawyer's trust account in Pennsylvania had bounced? Do banks normally hold funds for more than three or four days on checks over 10,000 dollars? If my inheritance check was not a valid deposit in my bank account, I realized, then the $3,000 check I had written paying off my Visa Card balance would also "bounce." There was a long pause at the ATM and then, thank goodness, it returned my bankcard. Had I inserted it upside down? I re-examined the little black magnetic strips on the back, looked again at the diagram showing exactly how to insert the card into the slot. Yes, I had performed my part of this modern wonder of technology correctly but still had no cash. And now I was worried. What else could be wrong with my bank account, I wondered as I headed south to Texarkana, hoping another ATM might be more productive.

Then, the surprise of geography for the day slapped me in the face as another huge sign welcomed us back to Texas at the Texarkana city limits! I had thought we would stay in Arkansas, but it was a bit of good fortune that we did not. Texas had big banking chains with ATMs all over including Texarkana, 600 miles from where we last entered this state near Dalhart. My cash request here was honored instantly, a perfunctory note thanked me for my business, and much to my relief, my balance indicated that the inheritance check was accepted as a deposit and the Visa Card payoff had been deducted. What a relief to know I was not on the shady side of the law, bouncing checks all over the country and perpetrating "unauthorized usages" on unsuspecting ATMs in Arkansas. Later, I asked another banker why he thought I received such a response from a cash machine. He said that was probably their standard message for any bank card which was not recognized as valid for that particular banks ATMs. The bank group in Arkansas was simply not affiliated with the national Cirrus or Plus card system.

Somewhere near Magnolia, Arkansas, I felt it was time to stop for lunch. All the money- chasing excitement this morning had made me hungry, and now I had the cash to blow at least three or four dollars for a meal. There was a roadside restaurant just off the highway that had food to go, served through a window, and there were picnic tables under some trees nearby. This was perfect for Pep and me on a bright, sunshiney day because it gave him a chance to run around while I ate, still being able to watch him and the motorcycle.

This particular stand served two items: fish and chicken, both fried, with a variety of side dishes and soft drinks. I chose the chicken because I am never quite sure what fish goes into those nebulous "fish bars," and this place was not winning any sanitary awards besides. As we ate, I tossed Pep the skins just to keep him from wandering too far from my table as he is prone to do when he gets bored or hungry. A dumpster behind the restaurant looked just like any ordinary trash receptacle, at a distance of about two hundred yards, until I saw a boy peek his head out the side door. Then, with a little heave and a jump, he was out and walking away. He had a stealthy look about him, always trying to see if anyone was staring at him or coming after him. It was my guess he was scrounging around for food or aluminum cans to peddle at the redemption center. I have seen street beggars in New York City going through the garbage cans in search of scraps outside a McDonald's restaurant, but never had I seen this out in the country. And we were surely out in the country. I had no idea what this little black boy's particular situation was, but once again, I felt fortunate to be as comfortable as I was.

El Dorado was the next good-sized city, 27,000 population, but I still could not find a Honda dealer with a tank bag for my bike. I had seen one in Denver with an 8 1/2 by 11 inch clear acetate sleeve for holding a full-sized map, which is the size of my Rand McNally atlas pages, each state on one page. After failing again at buying this hard to find item, I decided to wait until we got to Jacksonville, Florida, where one of the biggest Honda dealers in the country was located, and if any place would have one, they would. The *Wing World* magazine had one of their ads every month, touting their huge inventory of bikes and accessories. I always enjoy wandering through a place that caters to my weaknesses, even if I could not afford most of what they had for sale.

There were a lot of chicken farms in Arkansas- huge aluminum sheds that housed hundreds and hundreds of feeding chickens. Other sheds were used for incubating and hatching, but it looked like the biggest sheds were for growing chickens to a marketable size. When you think about how much chicken is consumed in this country every day, it is amazing to me that there are not more chicken farms. Almost every town in every state has some beef cattle, evident from the roadside, but in all my back road wanderings, I saw chicken farms only in Arkansas and Alabama. Maybe the fact that chickens are concentrated in sheds while cattle tend to roam all over a farm's acreage might account for their less conspicuous presence.

     Route 82 in Arkansas dead ended just past Crossett, at the intersection of State Highway 81. A right-hand turn took us south for eight miles into Louisiana. I forget who welcomed us into this state, but it was not Governor Edwin Edwards as I had anticipated. Maybe this road was not big enough to warrant any welcome sign other than the official state line pronouncement, which does not have to be changed every time there's a change in the governor's office. Governor Edwards was the first elected official I could ever remember admitting that he liked to gamble, to drink good southern whiskey, and to enjoy a number of different girlfriends now and then. He said on "60 Minutes" that his constituents admired his honesty, but the commentator suggested that running against avowed Klu Klux Klan leader David Duke didn't hurt him either. Nevertheless, he did not pretend to be a person of different morals than he actually was. And as a result, it would be hard to find any "skeletons in the closet" after the elections because all the revelations had already been made, without a tinge of regret I might add.

There was an enormous truck stop at the intersection of Louisiana 165 and Interstate 20 in Monroe, one of the major cities in the northern part of the state. I wanted to refuel at the end of the day and get a recommendation for a nearby campsite. The place was booming with truckers who not only bought fuel, but who also could eat at the cafeteria, wash their trucks with the jet steamers, and then take a shower themselves. Since they were so busy, and I was not really pushed for time, I took a while just to look at all the goodies. Every kind of radar detector, auto and truck parts, knives and billy sticks, handcuffs and stun guns crowded the shelves. Then I saw my favorite for disgusting laughs, "Betty Trucker's Road Kill Helper", a quasi-food item packaged with the same colors and lettering to closely resemble "Betty Crocker's Hamburger Helper." "Just add Possum, Rabbit, Coon, or Squirrel" the directions said. "Makes Any Meal Come Alive With Flavor" in a double entendre. Then in smaller print, " Not Recommended for Dog or Cat, (unless you don't tell your guests what they're eating)." The idea was so revolting to think about eating their "recommended" dishes much less the "not recommended" ones, I chuckled out loud. If I had room to carry a totally non-essential box for another three weeks, I might have even purchased the "Road Kill Helper" as a souvenir from Louisiana, although in all fairness, I later saw the same sick-humor package in other states too.

The cashier gave me directions to the Monroe Campground which was located right off I-20, only a couple of miles from their store. Numerous RVs were visible from the frontage road, and I fully expected to see a campground manager ringing up his cash register with all the new people checking in at 5 o'clock. Much to my surprise, however, the door to the office was locked and there was nobody anywhere except other camper and trailer owners. I waited around for a while sharing with the other would-be renters what our choices were. Finally, a lady who said she had lived in the park a long time told us to go find a site we liked, and the manager would come around later to collect the fees. So that's what we did. I found a site not far from the wash room, set up the tent for the night, fed Pep, and went to clean up myself. The door was locked and a clearly-lettered sign said "This Bathroom is for Campers Only. Be Sure to Turn Your Key in at the Manager's Office When You Leave." That was well and good if I had a key, but, of course, that would have to wait for the manager.

I then tied Pep up to the safety chain on the trailer and road out of the park to a nearby restaurant where I could use their restroom facilities and eat dinner too. It was about 7 o'clock when I got back from supper and I stopped at the manager's office again to see if anyone had returned. Not a thing had changed. The plate-glass window revealed his desk with a lamp turned on, papers spread out everywhere, a set of golf clubs standing up in the corner, a stuffed deer head mounted on the wall, but absolutely no activity. It looked as if he had run out expecting to be gone only a short time, but when I left the next morning, not one item had changed. I never could figure out why someone would just run off and leave his business at a crucial time, but that's the way it was at the Monroe Campground that Saturday night in October. Maybe I'll get a bill from someone after they read this chapter of the book.

Day 16: LOUISIANA

When I started to share some ideas with my wife about writing my chronicles of this trip, she opined that most books today don't have wide appeal without a regular dose of sex and violence. I replied that this book would have to be doomed to the ranks of the unappealing then because there just were not any incidents of that type during my travels with Peppy. My closest "call," however, came this morning as we left Monroe, Louisiana.

It seemed like a good idea to ride for a while before stopping for breakfast. I wanted to sort out my thoughts on the Monroe Campground while I scouted a good place to eat. The carefree timetable got moved up a bit though when it started to sprinkle. Light rain and overcast skies made the Waffle Shop more appealing than usual when we pulled off after only 10 or 15 miles. I tied Pep underneath the eaves of the building where he would be out of the rain, and I could still see him from inside. My motorcycle and trailer were also visible from my table as I ordered my favorite, a pecan waffle with strawberries on top. My waitress was a very business-like gal who seemed to be flying all around taking orders and delivering food to the other customers. Another waitress, a younger girl with sort of wind-blown, honey colored hair breezed by, stopping only long enough to say that she really liked my bike and that her "Daddy rides one just like it, a big red

Honda GoldWing, really nice." I thanked her for the compliment and briefly mentioned that we were on a cross-country trip from Colorado, camping out along the way, and heading east from here. "Wow, that sounds exciting!", she said as she sprinted off to take another food order at a distant table. Later, when I was finished with my breakfast, I went back to use the men's room before leaving the place. In the hallway to both the men's and ladies' rooms, this same waitress was getting ready to change out of her uniform at the end of her shift, but instead of waiting until she was inside the ladies' restroom, she started to undo her scarf and blouse as she talked to me. "You know, I just love motorcycles. When my Daddy first taught me to ride, I had to stand on my tippy toes to reach the ground," as she made a gesture indicating how far the seat came up against her crotch while trying to stand on the tips of her toes.

"Yes," I said, "my wife has short legs, too, makes it difficult to ride the big bikes."

"I don't think I could ride one like yours all by myself," she said, "but I really love being on one. My boyfriend has a Harley," as she undid another button on her blouse. By now, I could see the top of her lacy bra as I turned to see if anyone else was coming through the doors down the hallway. There was no one, and I was so befuddled I did not know what to do or what to say or how to escape. She was standing between the men's room and me. I could not gracefully go past her as she leaned her left elbow against the wall, stretched up for support as one hand rested on her head, the other hand on her next button! What was going on here? (Or more importantly, what was coming off?) There may have been a time in my younger years when this situation was all I could dream for, but now, as a happily married, middle aged man, I had no desire to do anything which would compromise my wonderful relationship with Sandy. With all the determination my red blood corpuscles could muster, I gently squeezed myself between the left wall and her right side, facing me, as I moved to the men's room. In silence, I closed the door, breathing hard and totally perplexed about what had happened, or was it just my over-active imagination? I must have spent a full 10 minutes in the bathroom because when I came out, the ladies room door was ajar, no signs of the wanton waitress in the restaurant proper, and there was a clear pathway to my bike, which I could not get on fast enough. As I think back on that encounter even now, I am perplexed about whether she was just so laid back and casual as to be indiscreet about starting to undress or whether she was making a pass for me. Regardless, if that was her normal behavior mode, she's begging for a lot of trouble before she's even old enough to handle it, in my humble but chaste opinion.

      The overcast morning continued as we approached the mighty Mississippi River. Tallulah, and then Mound, were the last towns in Louisiana as we started to ascend the aging metal bridge, our link to Vicksburg, Mississippi. Near the top of the bridge, I was somewhat disappointed that the biggest river in the country was not wider and grander at this historical crossing point. It seemed to be only a hundred feet wide with some small trees growing into the banks on both east and west sides. Then the bridge continued a little further, and the entire panorama that is the Mississippi River opened up in front of me. I had wrongly supposed that the old meandering of former river channels was the main body of the river itself only to be amazed again at how wide and magnificent this waterway really is. Barges and tugboats slowly made their way up and down the river as we passed by, about a hundred feet above. The metal crisscross pattern of the steel strips made motorcycle travel both loud and shaky. I could not do much sight seeing as I tried to concentrate on keeping the bike pointed straight ahead. A light motorcycle, particularly with knobby tires for off-road riding, would not have been able to make this crossing. The gaps in the ribbons of bridge steel might throw a dirt bike over. It was hazardous and unstable, even for a heavy GoldWing with smooth touring tires.

The city of Vicksburg is steeped in Civil War history. There is a National Monument, covering several hundred acres on the east side, with markers of all the different divisions from the various states whose loyal sons were lost in the battles waged there. From April to July, 1863, Union forces under the command of General Ulysses S. Grant laid siege to the Confederate stronghold commanded by General John C. Pemberton, who finally surrendered on July 4, 1863. It was a critical battle in the war because the Union victory gave them control of the Mississippi River and split the Confederacy in two. Vicksburg's capture, combined with the Union success at Gettysburg (July 1863), shifted the impetus of victory to the North. Historical markers everywhere commemorate all the deaths and struggles of 130 years ago. All the buildings in the "Old Town" have been, or are being, restored to the architecture of that period, semi-Victorian gingerbread. I rode around the waterfront for about half an hour just to see all the historic sites and renovations underway. Vicksburg may have lost that particular battle years ago, but ancestors of those southerners are capitalizing on the tourism today, making the Natchez-Vicksburg the fastest growing area in Mississippi. In a state that is still basically poor, ranked # 50 in median family income of $24,448 per year, tourist dollars are welcomed and cultivated. Granted, magnolias are nice and southern gentility culturally correct, but neither adds to the economy as much as the motel, gift shop, and restaurant revenues from those (Yankee) tourists.

    The ride across the rest of Mississippi was fairly uneventful. It was still alternating between being overcast and dry to light showers with real honest to goodness rain. I had my rain gear on once, but it was almost impossible to walk around a rest area with all that stiff yellow vinyl covering chaps and a leather jacket, so I decided to let the mist linger on my riding clothes. It never really penetrated the outer layer or I would have covered up with the waterproofs again. When the weather is damp, as it often was in Mississippi with an average annual precipitation of 53 inches, I try to concentrate on just moving rather than making good time. I had no deadline to meet, but I had hoped to get hold of my ex-brother-in-law who still lived in south Alabama, near Dothan, in order to see if we could get together tomorrow. Unfortunately, I only had an old phone number from when he was married, and now he was divorced and living somewhere else on his own. Apologetically, I called his former wife to explain my situation and see if she had Charley's current phone number. She was very cooperative but said that the only number she had was at his office, a state employment agency, a since today was Sunday, everything was closed. Also, since tomorrow was Columbus Day, a recognized holiday in Alabama, the office would not be open then either. She suggested I call directory information in Ozark, Alabama, to see if they had a listing for Charley Atkins. I thanked her for her help realizing that the conversation was a strain under the circumstances. I would try to get Charley's number later, when I was in Alabama. My plan right now was to reach to Montgomery by the end of the day.

    Our next stop was a beautiful wooded, rest area east of Meridian, Mississippi. It was still drizzling so we probably stopped more often than normal with slick roads that required a constant cleaning of windshields and face masks. As I pulled in to the parking area there was a big black Kawasaki Voyager touring bike with some unusual decals and pin striping. The owner was not around, but I left the GoldWing next to it and hiked up the hill to the tourist center, hoping this was one of those places that served complimentary hot coffee to travelers. Southern hospitality was very limited here. No hostesses were on duty and the coffee vending machine was taking quarters without giving any hot drinks in return. A big man with a heavy brown poncho that came down to his knees was getting ready to arm-wrestle the whole vending machine when I came up. Sure enough, he was riding a Kawasaki, and no, he didn't mind if I tried to get a cup of coffee too. My quarters worked fine which seemed to irritate the biker all the more. He finally agreed to try one more time, with one of my quarters, and thankfully for the vending machine, it gave him a cup of coffee. He was a retired army sergeant who didn't mince words and had an opinion on everything. "Never would buy one of those GoldWings. They want too much money for the name "Honda." My Kawasaki is just as good and I paid $2,000 less for it. Those Honda people just won't deal, and I don't like getting screwed. I've been buying and riding bikes for 30 years." Sensing his machismo, I asked if he had ever run into any trouble during his travels.

"Nothing I couldn't handle," as he pulled out a semi-automatic pistol from a shoulder holster under his rain gear. "And I carry another one on the bike, just for backup." I didn't ask, but he spoke as if he had used them more than once and would again on the slightest provocation. "You got to watch out for them niggers around here, they're always out to get you, especially the uppity ones." There was no doubt about his prejudices, and as he rode away, with Alabama tags on his bike, I imagined that the "Deep South" is going to have to wait another generation before racial hatred and bigotry among the less educated whites subsides. Pep and I could not solve all the problems of the world today, however, since we too were on our way to Alabama and crossed the line about an hour later at Cuba, population 486. I remember the town because that is where we turned off I-20, I-59 and headed straight east for Montgomery on Highway 80. From there, we passed through the city of Demopolis and then Selma about an hour later. Anyone who was an adult in the 1960s remembers Dr. Martin Luther King and his civil rights march on Selma. Next to the police confrontations with protesters in Birmingham, this is my most vivid recollection of the Deep South from this period. Later, I would learn that those sentiments causing racial tension were still alive and well in many parts of the state and with many people whom you would not expect to harbor such shallow feelings.

The K.O.A. in Montgomery was my travel goal for this day, and I was happy to find the place before 5 p.m. that Sunday afternoon. The manager was a sort of suspicious guy who was always looking at everyone, both inside and outside, with comments wondering what they were up to. "You just passing through?" he asked. "Where you from? Where you going?" in a tone more than curious but not quite like police questioning. "From Colorado, heading to Florida right now," I replied. "You on vacation, or got business down there, if you don't mind my asking." I don't think it mattered whether I mind or not, I could tell there was no stopping his inquisition.

"A little of both," I said, "you see, I'm writing a story about this trip, with the dog and all, on a motorcycle. It's probably not every day you have this combination here, is it?"

"No, it ain't. Can't say that I've ever had one just like you, although we get a lot of bikers in the summer, and almost every trailer here has a dog with it." Finally, he satisfied himself with my registration information, charge card for payment, and general character enough to show me a campsite. I needed to ask about a place to eat dinner in an hour or so, but I had the distinct impression that he was going to tell me more than I wanted to know. So instead, I waited for his wife who directed me to the nearest Western Sizzling. At least the campsite was level, and it was quiet enough for both Pep and me to get a good night's sleep without having to wonder if the manager was coming home anytime soon.

Day 17: ALABAMA

I have a bunch of memories about Alabama, most of them bad. My first wife and I moved back to her hometown, Gadsden, after her father died in the fall of 1978. He had owned and operated a small accounting machine business at the time of his death, and, on the way back to Florida after his funeral, my wife begged me to consider buying her late father's business from her mother allowing us and our three children to move back to Alabama. She wanted to be near her grieving mother, she thought Gadsden would be a place to raise the children, and I honestly thought I could make a success of the business machines company. After all, I had been successful with Xerox Corporation several years earlier, and the idea of being my own boss certainly did appeal to me. On the downside, however, I had been with Merrill Lynch six years at that point and I hated to give up all my customer base which was the source of my comfortable, but not outstanding, livelihood. But something else made me hesitate. Visiting with her family in Alabama over the 13 years we had been married always gave me the impression we were almost in another country more than another state. Everyone spoke with a real southern drawl, their daily activities were so slow motion as to appear to be half-speed with half-energy, and it just seemed like a closed society; if you were not born and raised there, you were a different breed of cat, not likely to be accepted without long periods of personal sniff tests. Nevertheless, after a few days of consideration coupled with lots of tugging at the heart strings, we decided to up and move there so I could buy the small family business. Within two weeks after resigning from Merrill Lynch and selling our house in Florida, my mother-in-law turned from a sickly sweet, doting grandmother type into a violent shrew who would plunge into fits of anger, screaming at anyone in sight who happened to not be able to get out of the way when she felt particularly put upon. Time after time she would alternate between crying and yelling about how no living human being had ever had such a difficult situation as that she was in. Worse, *everybody*, including my wife and I, were out to screw her, a poor widow, in the most devious of ways. One time, at my new business only a couple of weeks, all the daily mail was opened by the secretary receptionist who realized, too late, that one oil company credit card bill belonged to my late father-in-law and was not a company expense. I gave it to my mother-in-law that evening without even thinking and she flew into a rage, ranting about how it was a sign of my "poor breeding" that I would open someone else's personal mail. AND, she advised me, it was a FEDERAL OFFENSE, for which she could have me arrested by the F.B.I. Nothing I could apologize for had any diminishing effect on the gravity of this situation in her mind. Unfortunately, I tried to have my wife intercede for me but that simply put both of us on her list of despicable, no account human beings, a position from which I will not live long enough to ever rise above. Another time, at our house in Gadsden much later, she threw open the kitchen door at supper time, and in front of my wife and children, accused me of stealing her oxblood shoe polish out of their shoe shine box when I had stayed there 2 or 3 months ago. She knew it was I because nobody else would do such a thing unless they were a (damn) Yankee. I offered to go to the drug store, right then and there, to buy her a new can of oxblood shoe polish if that would please her. Of course, she said that I missed the whole point which was not the missing shoe polish but rather that I was such a "low life person" to have done such a thing in the first place and then stormed out of our house with the same fury she had entered only minutes earlier. My whole family and I discussed "Grandmama Jean's" problem and decided we would just try to avoid her for a while and hope that she mellowed in time. That was never to be. My first wife and I got divorced a couple of years later, and when I left Alabama to go back to work for Merrill Lynch in Florida, Grandmama Jean still hated me enough to file a lawsuit trying to garnish my wages, not for my ex-wife and children (to whom I was paying support), but for her because of all her "pain and suffering" at having to deal with me. My own parents thought my ex-mother-in law had lost some of her marbles at that time in her life and there was nothing any of us could do about her depression and rage fits. In retrospect, I tend to think they were right. It is the only time or place in my entire life that someone has continually and categorically accused me of having "bad breeding" as the root of all my shortcomings, of which there are admittedly many. As a matter of fact, it is only in Alabama that I ever even heard the term "breeding" in reference to a person's character or virtuosity. In my own childhood, I had always heard the term "good breeding" in reference to cows or bulls for a dairy farm, never with regard to a human being's grace or manners.

There were other things about Alabama that contributed to my unhappy recollections. I lived there only for three years and I developed some wonderful friendships with a few relaxed and good natured people. Nevertheless, the underlying currents of racial superiority by most of the whites, the general lack of spending on education in the public arena, the continual references to the Confederacy and the South as a symbol of a bygone and supermost virtuous era, the contrasting denigration of the North in general and Yankees (and me) in particular, the "Bear Bryant" religion at the University of Alabama football team, the George-Wallace mentality that allowed him to bypass the state constitution in order to serve four non-consecutive terms as governor and populist hero, and finally, a lack of tolerance for anyone who does not hold the same intensity of feeling on these matters, all contribute to making most outsiders want to stay that way.

Like a breath of fresh air, however, my ex-brother-in-law, Charley, had the rare ability to poke fun at almost everything and everybody, including his mother, himself, and me, with such wit and charm as to be my most favorite person in the entire state. Once, at the dinner table a couple of months after Mr.Atkins had died, Grandmama Jean was agonizing over how to possibly get all the thank-you letters written to all the good people who had come to the funeral and brought food to the grief party afterwards. She wailed on and on about how long it was going to take to write all the personal letters expressing her gratitude for their sympathy. Finally, when all of us could not stand to hear any more, Charlie said "Mama, why don't you just take out a big ad in the *Gadsden Times*, put Daddy's picture in there, and tell everyone how much you appreciate their sympathy." It was comic relief at its best, and I was so glad he said it and not I. His mother gasped, "Oh Charley, that is so uncouth, I don't know how you could say such a thing. Only trashy people put ads in the paper like that." On another occasion about the same time period, Grandmama Jean was wondering out loud what would be the best epitaph for her late husband's tombstone, "should I put a scripture from the book of St. Matthew or a poetic verse from Shakespeare?" Once again Charley came up with the classic suggestion to take the edge off of a melodramatic moment " Mama, the thing that Daddy would most want to have over his body, without any doubt in my mind, is 'Roll Tide Roll.'" It was so funny because it was so true. There was no greater Alabama football fan anywhere on the face of the earth than Lon Atkins. In victory, he would drink himself to a blind jubilation; in defeat, I have seen him slam the door as he stormed out of the house, not to be seen or heard from for two days while he nursed his psychological wounds through recovery and back to normalcy. He was in love with "the team" and drew such vicarious pleasure from its successes, and such personal devastation from its failures, that it truly was a part of his life and his personality. The equally interesting phenomena is that Lon was not alone. Although I did not personally know any other super fanatical fans, there were stories in the paper almost every day in the fall about the ends to which some men (boys) had gone to express their joy or their rage. Domestic violence and even murders after an Alabama football game loss were not uncommon. It added new meaning to the term "sportsfan."

These memories were my recollection as I traveled toward Dothan from Montgomery that Monday morning, hoping to be able to reach Charley on the phone and maybe even visit with him for a while. As his ex-wife had suggested, I called information in Ozark, Alabama and asked for a listing of Charles H. Atkins, his full and proper name. The operator said she had no listing for that exact name, but she did have a "Charley Atkins" and gave me the number. When I called it, however, I got a message on the answering machine sounding like some destitute sharecropper, "Weez ain't home richt now but if you'z jez leave ya numba, I'z get bak to y'all real zoon." I didn't have the courage to leave a name or a number not knowing if Charley had a joke recording or if, in fact, it really was some poor black man's home. I tried his office a couple of times later in the trip, but he was either not there or tied up with someone in a meeting, and I had no way to leave a return number. Whenever we talk again though, I'm sure it will be a festive reunion, and I definitely will send him a copy of my chronicles.

Just eleven miles south of Dothan, we crossed the border into Florida and continued south to intersect with I-10, the southernmost transcontinental interstate. As far as Florida travel is concerned, I-10 connects Pensacola with Tallahassee and continues east to Jacksonville in a band across the northern part of the state. Since all major roads to south Florida connect with I-10, it is an important tourist artery, and tourism is Florida's biggest industry, hitting ten billion dollars a year, more than any other state. It is not surprising, therefore, that when several incidents of tourists being robbed, raped, and murdered hit the national and international headlines, the State of Florida said enough is enough and something had to be done to counterbalance this new found and terribly negative image.

The very first rest area on I-10 displayed Florida's answer to thugs and hoodlums, "This Area is Patrolled by Armed Guards 24 Hours a Day." The signs were not only at the turn offs from the interstate, they were all over the rest area itself. Even more of a deterrent to the would be criminals, however, was the visible presence of uniformed guards with big handguns and walkie talkies constantly walking around the grounds. I talked to one of them about the increased security effort. He said it was more of a public relations campaign than an actual response to high crime since there had been only three or four incidents in the entire state, but each one received more press than the previous one and the state really wanted to counteract the negative publicity. He admitted that for the most part his job was really boring. (The most exciting confrontation he had experienced so far was asking two homosexuals to leave the men's rest room where they were both in the same stall and another guest had complained something unusual was going on.) He had been hired right out of law enforcement vocational training school four months ago by Wackenhut Security, the big Florida firm under contract with the state for this program. They were patrolling all the rest areas on every major highway in the entire state, from Key West to Pensacola, over 460 miles. I don't know how much all these extra guards cost the Florida legislature, but I do know that it had to be a bundle, and the fear of losing the tax revenues on 10 billion dollars of tourism was a stronger motivation than any concern for the public welfare. After all, as the late Senator Everett Dirkson said one day on the floor of the House of Representatives, "A billion dollars here, a billion dollars there, and pretty soon, you're talking about real money."

As much as the Florida coastline, with all its oceanfront beaches and condominiums, is appealing to a wide variety of tourists, plus Disney World around the Orlando area, the interior highways are almost all flat and straight, mile after mile. At least there are some rolling hills in north Florida to break up the monotony of the road, and Pep and I pulled into a campground near Tallahassee just a little after 6 that afternoon having covered just less than 300 miles due to our long stops in Dothan. This park, more than any other I would see on the trip, was also a storage place for lots and lots of inactive RVs and trailers, for one reason or another out of favor with their owners' current recreational requirements. It was a bit like spending the night in a cemetery, but neither Pep nor I had any trouble going to sleep that night, he because all the scampering squirrels had worn his hind end to a frazzle, and me because I was not going to be arrested for having "bad breeding" in Florida.

Day 18: FLORIDA

Our campground seemed to have more bugs in the morning than it had the night before. It was probably just my perception, but there was no breeze, and the sun was already warming me up to a sweat as I folded down the camper and got some fresh water for Pep. This was strictly a place to park, for only six dollars a night, so breakfast would have to wait until our first stop. The humidity was higher here than any place we had been so far, and I could see Pep's tongue hanging out as he bounded into his kennel, the last action prior to take off. Rather than get back on the interstate this morning, I decided to ride on Highway 90 which ran roughly parallel, and I could get back on halfway across the state if need be.

This was a good decision since the first town, Monticello, also had a wonderful restaurant with an all-you-can-eat breakfast bar that would hold me over until dinner. Huge servings of scrambled eggs, bacon, sausage, cinnamon rolls, and grits with gravy overloaded my cholesterol intake for the day and it was only 8 o'clock! The waitress here, unlike the waif at the Waffle Shop back in Louisiana, was as wide as she was tall, but still very pleasant, and she offered me a ham hock bone for Pep after she found out who he belonged to. I waddled out of the place positive that I had gotten my $5.95 worth and could only get sick if I tried for more. Pep was delighted to chew on that bone nearly the entire day, and I managed to start breathing normally again by the time we got to Live Oak, another 70 miles down the road. The highway we were on was the original east-west road long before the interstate was built; I enjoyed seeing the 1950s-style motels and small towns. About this time on our trip, my less than a year old Minolta Maxxum autofocus camera started acting up, only firing shots when it wanted to which was becoming less and less often for some reason unknown to me. So when I saw a large pawn shop in Live Oak with a sign advertising cameras in the same size letters as handguns, I thought it must have been their specialty, and they might be able to tell me what was wrong with mine. The man who ran the shop was tied up telling some young black woman why her wedding and engagement rings weren't worth very much in pawn, so his wife tried to see if she could help me. Unfortunately, she said that her husband really did not know that much about cameras, he just took them in on pawn based on their "book value," taken from a little blue book which had listings on every gun in the world, plus cameras, jewelry, and musical instruments. The young woman customer soon walked out in disgust at the pawnbroker's offer, and he turned his attention to me. What his wife said was true, his specialty was guns, not cameras, but he did have a replacement lithium battery which we tried in the camera to see if that made it jump back to life. No such luck, it was still not willing to click and blink, even with a fresh power source. I thanked him for his time and effort, told him I didn't need a another gun today, and soon we were back on main street, heading east. When we were not on a freeway, I would stop at parks near the center of town for Pep to take care of business while we went for a walk. Although this was the twelfth of October, it felt like the middle of summer in temperature and humidity. After living in Colorado for five years, I think both Pep and I had gotten used to the dry cool climate and preferred it over the heat and humidity.

Originally, I had planned to go down to South Florida where I had lived for most of the 1970s and where my parents still lived, but they had gone up to New England for the summer and were not yet back. It was too far to travel just to see some old friends and then turn right around and come back north again on the same roads for 250 to 300 miles. I decided to continue east to Jacksonville where I was sure I could find a tank bag for my motorcycle and then find a place to camp for the night.

Although we were only about 25 miles from the Gulf of Mexico in Tallahassee, I didn't actually see the coast there so this stopover in Jacksonville would be my first glimpse of the Atlantic Ocean, a sight I hadn't seen in a couple of years. The Osceola National Forest north of Lake City provided another scenic rest area, also with armed guard patrols, for a mid-way point on the road east. The forests in Florida are not at all like those of the Pacific Northwest. The pine trees either don't grow as big or they have all just been cut down in the last 20 years because none of the forestation has the size of trees in the north. What they lack in dimensions, however, they make up for in density. The natural woods in this part of Florida is almost like a jungle, the trees and vegetation are so thick. Even here the climate is subtropical with an average annual temperature in the high 60s, 53 degrees in January and 81 degrees in July. The Florida Keys are actually the only place in Florida and, indeed, in the country, with a true tropical climate averaging 71 degrees in January and 84 degrees in July. Yet the whole state is blessed with gentle breezes (most of the time) from the Gulf Stream, and today was no exception.

We got back on I-10 about 20 miles past Lake City in the early afternoon. The timing seemed to be working out perfectly for me to be able to ride to "Honda of Jacksonville," buy a tank touring bag, drool over all the brand-new GoldWings, and then continue up the coast to an interesting park for the night. That's almost the way it turned out.

Jacksonville is the largest city in Florida with a population of 673,000 as of the 1990 census. We had not been in a city of any size since Albuquerque and that seemed like light years ago. The skyline was a majestic panorama of tall buildings bordered by the St. Johns River, the only major body of water in the country which flows north. Just as in Denver, the population of the city proper belies the metro population which, in both cases, more than doubles the actual number of people living and working in the area.

I studied my detail map in vain, trying to figure out how to get from the 285 Beltway to Atlantic Boulevard, the street on which Jacksonville Honda was located. Just at that time, a police officer happened to pull into the same convenience store parking lot where I was pondering the map. He was one of those law enforcement types who prided himself not only on knowing where everything is in the city, but he also wanted to see how quickly he could get it out of his mouth, as if he were talking to a dispatcher over the radio. I tried to copy the directions as he slowed down to bursts of ten knots from his original twenty five, "I-10 to I-95, north to Union Street, straight over the maroon bridge, the Regency Mall on your left, bear to your right to Atlantic and Jacksonville Honda will be on your left, a couple of miles up the boulevard," and the those infamous words of assurance, "you can't miss it." Almost an hour later, I had Jacksonville Honda on the pay phone trying to get directions from them how to get to their shop from the other (wrong) side of the Regency Mall. "How did you get over there," the parts manager asked? Never mind that Jacksonville's finest had steered me to exactly where I was, "just give me the simplest way to your shop," I demanded. All this worthless street meandering had now cut into my beach sight seeing time and I was a little frustrated over not being able to find the place. Finally, we pulled into their huge parking lot and both Pep and I heaved a sigh of relief. Yes, they surely did have tank bags "only $115, but they last a lifetime." "Don't you have any that will last only 5 or 10 years for a little less?" "Nope, that's our only tank bag for the GoldWing 1200, unless you want to go to this bigger Markland model over here for $185, on sale." It always happens, somehow I now felt like I was getting a good deal on the bag I originally thought was outrageously over priced. I had struggled so long without my maps at close hand during this trip, I really wanted to be able to easily see where I was going, they had the perfect tank bag,... what's a few more dollars in the overall scheme of the universe? Who will care five years from now? I gave him my credit card and started my gasping at the new GoldWings nearby while he processed my sale through the store computer which in turn talked to the bank card computers. I had already decided how to spend another $18,000 by the time he finished with my first $120. "Here put this 1994 Teal GoldWing Special Edition with color coordinated matching trailer on my Visa Card." I could just see his eyes popping at the prospect of a commission on such a big and unforeseen sale. The computer would strain its chips and diodes to process those monster numbers in nanoseconds. We would wait for what seems like an eternity while the whirring and clicking continued, until finally, the inevitable message gloated, "This transaction exceeds your credit limit. Please contact your bank." "Okay," I would then say "do you take CASH?" His eyes would pop one more time as he tried to figure out whether I was a drug dealer or just a fool. "Just kidding" I would say, as he pushed me out of the store for titillating with his emotions over something as serious as a big motorcycle sale.

    Oh well, it's fun to dream. After all, fantasy is not a vice, is it? Maybe, but as Abraham Lincoln said, "A man without any vices usually doesn't have any virtues either." So Pep and I were in noble spirits as we stopped to walk along the Atlantic and Neptune beaches late that afternoon. It was going to be rush hour traffic soon, though, so I rode over the Saint John's River one last time, past Quarantine Island and Mayport Naval Station on our way north to Georgia. There was only a short stretch where the commuter traffic on I-95 was a slow-flow problem and then it opened up as the Peach State welcomed us.

    I had been to Sea Island a couple of times for family reunions and knew how beautiful this coastal resort part of Georgia could be. Jimmy Carter had frequented St. Simons Island during his presidency so I felt in pretty good company as we turned into Blythe Island Regional Park in Brunswick, Georgia. The ranger gave me a map of the grounds and since it was almost closing time, he also gave me the combination to the lock at the main gate which they closed every evening at dusk for the protection of the campers and the park facilities. I could not have asked for a better, more picturesque setting on the entire east coast. It was our own private wooded preserve with trails and lagoons for an early evening stroll. Peppy felt inclined to take a dip in the water after a long hot day which did not bother me until I thought about the alligators. Years ago, when we lived in Florida, I had let my dog go for a swim in a similar lake area in the Everglades. While "Boris" was retrieving a stick I had thrown, an Indian fisherman pointed out to me that the brown hump drifting over this way was really an alligator's head, and he had his eyes on my dog for certain. I frantically called Boris out of the water just as the "log" floated close enough to have killed him with those powerful jaws. The more I remembered that incident, particularly how stealthy the gator was, I decided Pep, too, could forego the swim in favor of caution. We walked back to the campsite, I left him on guard while I washed some clothes for the first time in a week, and managed to find a nearby cafe for dinner, in between laundry cycles. We went to sleep listening to the hoots and cackles of birds in the swampy woods, and no unwelcomed guests.

Hot Arizona Property:
Adorable Adobe Hacienda

Santa Fe Mission: Home of
the Padres.

Day 19: GEORGIA & the CAROLINAS

One of the advantages of being assigned a camp site near the community rest rooms is that it is so convenient for washing, showering, and using the john. The disadvantage to this location, I found out this morning, is that other campers do the same thing...so do their children, loud, playful, and excited children. I woke up to Pep barking as the juvenile delinquents-in-training made their way past my camper and onto the trail leading to the rest rooms, pointing and daring each other to approach Pep.

"Look at that dog. Is he vicious or what?" one said to the other.

"Yea, why don't you go pet him Billy. He wouldn't bite you. Ha.Ha."

"Not me, why don't you go Jeffy Baby."

I quickly put on my jeans and jumped out of the tent to calm Pep down who, by this point, had worked himself into his killer-dog charade, lunging and straining at his leash with lips snarling up showing his fangs, pretending to be much tougher than he in fact ever had been.

"Hey mister, does your dog bite?" the older boy asked.

"Yes, he does sometimes. Not very hard though. Here, I'll let him loose to see if he can catch one of you."

"No...No...oh...oh, let's get out of here" as they ran down the wooded path to the safety of a door that closed behind them. I took Pep for a walk in the other direction, back to the lagoon we had visited yesterday, for a chance to do his business before we left. I didn't see the boys again although I rode by several camps on my way out that had enough noise to have been part of their group. I always enjoy teasing youngsters to see what their reactions are to unexpected situations, without ever putting real fear into them. I was such a juvenile delinquent myself that it sort of brings back fond memories of yesteryear. I have no idea what they told their parents, however, so it's probably a good thing I didn't see them again.

"There he is Dad! That's the man with the wolf that almost killed Billy and me."

The ranger station at the entrance to the park had a more talkative type this morning as I went to check out. She wanted to know if my stay had been pleasant and would I mind filling out a comment card for their evaluation later. I happily complied with her request and faulted only the laundry room where one of the washing machines was jammed with a slug or foreign coin thereby allowing only one load at a time in the second washer. Since I had advanced to the laundry-skill level where I separated my dark jeans and clothes from my white underwear and sweatshirts, it took twice as long to get the wash done last night. She apologized for the inconvenience and said she would put in a call for service to the Laundromat vendor. Overall, however, I told her that Blythe Island Regional Park was one of the most beautiful camping facilities I had seen in all my travels and gave her my stock photo souvenir of Pep and me at Lake Dillon. Without exception, everyone who looked at that picture, which is also on this book cover, said they remembered how magnificent the mountains were in Colorado *or* that they wanted to go there sometime in their own travels. While she was studying the picture, another giant sized RV pulled up to check out. The older man and his wife just gushed over how cute Pep was and what an interesting combination we made. "Could we take a picture of you and your dog, together?" Ah, the life of fame and fortune never gets old as we complied with yet another tourist request. The older lady, like many other people we met, asked if I had read John Steinbeck's novel, Travels With Charley, which ,of course, was my inspiration and partial motivation for this journey. If even only one person compares me to John Steinbeck *after* they have read my book, I will consider myself to have arrived in terms of literary circles. Regardless, I thoroughly enjoyed his book in the early 1960s, and the reference was enthusiastically received. Pep may not enjoy being compared to a poodle, Charley, but I *love* being compared to Steinbeck, even if he drove a pick up truck with a camper shell.

  I pulled into the Citgo gas station in Brunswick to refuel before leaving on what I knew was going to be a long distance day in Georgia and the Carolinas. Much to my chagrin, I noticed a dent in the right front corner of the trailer which I had not seen before. How could this have happened without my knowledge? Did someone back into it while it was parked at the camp site when I was out for dinner or laundry? But Pep was tied up to the safety chain. Had I, perhaps, hit some short post, only a foot high, and not even known what had happened? I never did figure out how that dent got there, at least 4 to 5 inches wide, but I was sure Larry could help me get it repaired when we got back to Denver.

    While we were at this gas station, pondering the dent, a group of laborers were waiting out front to be picked up for that day's jobs. When I came out of the store, after paying for my gas and coffee, they were all cheering and yelling at something along side the store's grassy area. I, too, poked my head around the corner only to see Pep, hell bent for leather chasing a rabbit who had the misfortune to run across the field as my dog was marking a bush. Every time the rabbit would make a fast turn, almost in the opposite direction, Pep would try to follow as his rear end drifted in the direction he had been running, almost causing him to slide around each corner. He was having the time of his life, at the expense of the poor rabbit who finally jumped into a thicket too dense for Pep to follow. With his heart beating 90 miles a minute, the workers cheered him one last time as I called him to go with me. He had put on a lively show for the crowd, and they enjoyed the life and death entertainment, as most of us do when it's not our life on the line.

    Today's travel ended up being the longest of my entire trip. I didn't realize that when we started out this morning, however. I just knew that last night I had spoken with my son at Virginia Tech. in Blacksburg, and if I didn't get there by tonight, Wednesday, I wasn't going to have much of a visit with him because he worked Thursday nights for a food and banquet catering firm and had classes during most of the day. He has done a terrific job balancing both his need for an income while at college and his commitment to stay in school, and hopefully, to graduate in the not too distant future. He has a lot of friends, most of whom he has known since high school, and five of them shared an apartment off campus. I had signed on as a co-guarantor for a security deposit, at the request of the landlord, along with the other fathers I was told. Therefore, it was with both anticipation and trepidation that I wanted to see how these living arrangements were working out after the boys had been there two years. But Virginia was still three states away. My next goal was to ride to Savannah before lunch, 120 miles up Interstate 95.

This October day in south Georgia was another perfect scenario for a touring motorcycle trip. The humidity was high, especially if you were walking around in the sun, but on a bike at 65 miles per hour, the sun felt good and the breeze evaporated any moisture on my skin. This road had not changed much since we had first moved to Florida twenty years ago. Town names stayed the same- Darien, South Newport, Richmond Hill, and finally Savannah. All had memories of traveling north and south for the holidays, a car full of kids wanting to know if we were there yet. I can't say as I blame them either. Car travel on the interstates can be pretty boring. The scenery all looks the same after a while, and hour after hour is the same as the one before. Not so on a motorcycle, however. A rider is always alert to his surroundings, in tune with the changing variables: sun or rain, wind or breeze, smooth road or rough, friendly traffic or hostile truck, straight road or construction detour? All have to be continually evaluated. Is this a potentially dangerous situation? Should I get out of the way? Should I slow down or swerve? Can I avoid a mistake on the part of another driver? These thoughts constantly raced through my mind, even as we cruise down a super highway at turnpike speeds, covering ground in giant leaps.

Savannah was here in no time and we pulled off only long enough to stretch our legs and have a bite to eat. Twenty minutes is enough time standing still in the Georgia sun, even in the fall. Fifteen miles after lunch we were in South Carolina, where "nothing could be finer." Almost. During long periods on the road, and especially on the interstates like today, I developed a problem with my right hand known as "Carpel Tunnel Syndrome," which produces an effect similar to having a leg or arm "fall asleep," a rather uncomfortable tingling sensation. It comes from a tension on the nerves in the hand and wrist after being compressed, or tense, for extended periods of time. At first, when Sandy and I went riding during the summer, I didn't know what it was or what caused it, but some of the other GoldWingers said they had the same tingling sensation problem, almost always in their right hand which is what "works" the throttle, continually holding pressure against the spring-loaded safety return. Without my friction lock "cruise control," I never could have taken any extended trip because Carpel Tunnel's minor irritation quickly becomes painful if not relieved. The cruise setting at least takes the pressure off the right hand from having to hold the throttle open at a given speed. It does not adjust itself for hills or changes in wind conditions like an electronic cruise control would, but I can set the friction lock in any gear, even first, and at any speed, a feature which the electronic cruise control does not allow. As a result, at least 5,000 miles of this trip were ridden on my "cruise."

We "cruised" into Columbia, a sparkling jewel of a city, and the largest in South Carolina. It is clean and modern, rising up from the miles and miles of flatland as surprisingly as a slap in the face. In addition to being the state capital, the city also has become the center for manufacturing, distribution, and health services in South Carolina. Most of the tourism dollars, however, are spent along the seacoast, in Charleston, Hilton Head, and Myrtle Beach. Charleston boasts the oldest public museum in the United States, although I might question that designation vis-a-vie Santa Fe, as well as other historic sites from colonial days and the Civil War, which started at Fort Sumter in Charleston Harbor. Golf and fishing are the primary drawing cards at Hilton Head and Myrtle Beach, neither of which are well suited to motorcycle travel with a dog, I might add.

Right after Columbia, I picked up Interstate 77 which would take us straight north through the rest of South Carolina, all of North Carolina, and into Virginia. We were covering a lot of ground today, and if that is the primary goal, you cannot beat the efficiency of limited access freeways. I would liked to have seen more of the historical sites in both North and South Carolina, but visiting my son at college, whom I had not seen for almost a year, was more important to me. After passing through Charlotte, North Carolina, near the border with South Carolina, it was only another 90 miles to the Virginia state line. The scenery here was more interesting as the Appalachian mountains and foothills roll into western North Carolina and southwestern Virginia. I passed a big tractor trailer truck whose brakes had gotten too hot or failed as he had steered onto the runaway truck ramp approaching Hillsville. A state trooper was already on the scene and both he and the driver had fire extinguishers out trying to cool the smoldering, overheated brakes. There was smoke and steam everywhere. It appeared that his cargo, heaping full and rounded on top, was a load of coal produced at one of the many mines in this region.

The intersection of I-77 with I-81 near Wytheville, Virginia, meant I was on my last leg for this day, which by now had become very dark. Almost 500 miles on my trip odometer meant we had come a long way already with about 60 more miles to Blacksburg, home of Virginia Tech. and my son Raymond's apartment. No need for dinner now since I wanted to take him out after he got off from his job at 9 p.m., "the early shift."

It was a little after 8 o'clock when I finally found the boys' apartment with the help of a room mate's directions. Pep seemed as relieved as I was that we were through traveling, a grand total of 563 miles and our record for any one day. If I had any doubt about where I was going to spend the night, that was quickly dispelled when I entered their apartment. Anywhere, I realized, would be cleaner, and probably safer, than this place. My worst fears were confirmed. A person could die from the diseases which were incubating in the kitchen. Dirty dishes and rotting leftovers were mixed with moldy utensils in the sink; a pizza box lay ripped open on the counter. The doors almost came off the broken hinges as they swung open; the carpeting, such as was left of it, had empty beer cans and cigarette butts mixed with dirty laundry, and magazines. A huge crater in the sheetrock wall of the "living room" gave testimony to a drunk student's frustration after a disappointing date. He just put his head right through the wall to release some pent-up anger, I was later told. All the furniture had been ripped apart, frames sagging from repeated beatings, and stuffing coming out where seams had been in calmer times. I needed to use the bathroom and one of his room mates directed me to Ray's. The toilet seat was broken crossways in two near the hinge so that any sit down operation also involved rough scratching on your buttocks, as if one might need more incentive to finish quickly. All bottles of shampoo, tubes of toothpaste, and other unmentionables had the tops off, strewn on the floor waiting to be or having just been stepped on, as they oozed their last bit of medicinal life. Ray still was not home. I looked into his bedroom, no sheets on the bed, just a mattress cover with a month's stench of body odor and what not on it. An unused condom was on the dresser, a used one on the floor. Should I be glad that he practiced some form of safe sex or appalled that he had no compunction to clean up after himself? No, this was not the night for any kind of lecturing as I heard the door to the apartment open. Ray was home, and we immediately left in his car to find me a motel and to eat dinner. At 22 years old, he was even taller than I had remembered him only a year earlier. Surely, he had stopped growing by now. I was just glad to see him alive and in good health, no small wonder considering the filth and squalor he sleeps in every night.

"Hey! I thought you'd be impressed," Ray said. "We actually *cleaned* it up because we knew you were coming. It looked really bad yesterday."

I could hardly express my gratitude, but it didn't matter. I was overjoyed to be with him again and hear how the other parts of his life were going.

Florida: The Police State!

Ray's Bemmer

Day 20: VIRGINIA

The Imperial Motel in Blacksburg, like the bargain motel in Gallup, New Mexico, seemed to be owned and managed by folks from India. My oldest brother, who has been to India several times for extended visits on sabbatical, told me there is a certain province where all the motel operators come from, a sort of profession or occupation indigenous to that part of the country. I never did understand exactly why that was the case, and no motel manager from India that I ever met spoke English well enough to have the discussion. I was always thrilled just to get a room, after confronting the language barrier. Nevertheless, it was a good clean room, no garbage on the floor, the toilet seats didn't feel like a wire brush on my backside, and there were no trophy holes in the walls from some student's stressful disappointment with his date. Yes, considering the alternative, it was a wonderful room.

As soon as Ray was through with his morning classes, about 10:30, we met back at his apartment for a quick ride on the bike and then lunch. He had never been on a big touring bike before and, of course, had never seen this motorcycle since we had not yet bought it when he was in Colorado last New Years.

"Hey Dad," Ray joked with his usual respect, "do you think this motorcycle can carry two fat asses like us?" I had unhooked the trailer purposely so the

GoldWing would not have the double task of pulling and carrying extra weight at the same time.

"Well, I don't know. Let's just see how she goes," I said, knowing full well that I had given rides to equally big "asses" before. The gross vehicle weight of this bike allowed 400 pounds of load capacity. I had been carrying an extra helmet hooked onto the back frame for just such an occasion, and for safety's sake, it fit Ray perfectly. I fired up the 1200cc engine as he climbed on the back seat. After a brief explanation about never putting your feet down, lean with me on the corners, and other basics, we were off on a loop around Blacksburg. I think Raymond enjoyed showing me the campus almost as much as I enjoyed accelerating up to 80 miles an hour on the 460 Bypass.

"Do you think this bike can handle our fat asses?" I asked as I shifted into fourth gear at 5000 rpm's. The front wheel almost jumped off the ground from all the torque.

"Hey Dad, this is really exhilarating!" he replied. I remember his exact words because that's about as close as he gets to actually paying a compliment or saying he was excited. It wouldn't be "cool" to gush with genuine enthusiasm. But I could tell he was thrilled, and so was I, showing off my new toy to one of my children who had always been difficult to impress.

We cruised back to his apartment and parked the bike so we could all go to lunch, including Peppy, in his car. I had honestly been a bit concerned to learn he had purchased a BMW last year on his modest college income, but when I saw what a 1976 BMW with over 200,000 miles on it actually looks like, it certainly was not extravagant. Rust seeped through every fender and his friend, "the mechanic," had rebuilt the whole car and sold it to him for $700. I must admit, it ran like a top for that small amount of money. Pep didn't mind sitting on a protruding spring in the back seat anyway. He was happy just to see Ray again and to be included in this part of the family reunion. I couldn't agree more myself.

Ray chose a restaurant named Burgin's for lunch, a kind of fancy submarine shop with a nostalgia motif. Having old bicycles hanging from the ceiling allowed them to charge $6.95 for a sandwich, which was fine with me. We talked about his classes (boring), his job (great boss), his long range goals (what to do tonight), and other members of our family (what they're up to). It was a good conversation for a 49-year-old father and his 22-year-old son. The rough edges were more than compensated for by the very sincere nature of a rare one-on-one. I only see each of my children about once a year now, due to the distance between Colorado and Virginia, where all three live. They usually come out west for a visit either over the Christmas holidays or during the summer, and it's always enjoyable to be with them again, regardless of the stages of their lives. I love and respect each one, more now than when they were children, although in different ways. Hopefully, they still feel a fatherly love for me, inspite of all my shortcomings.

We had tied Pep outside near Raymond's car, and he jumped around like we had been gone for days, instead of only an hour, when we came back. Ray always enjoys "juicing" him up even more with shouts of "Where have you been? Are you ready to go? Are you sure? Where's that other Puppy?" (Pep always looks around for another dog intruding on his territory whenever he hears the word "Puppy." It's an instant way to spook him up in alert anticipation of an encounter that is totally make believe.)

It was early afternoon now, and I had only 35 miles to travel in order to get to Roanoke, Virginia, where my other son, Dal, and his mother lived. Last night on the phone, I had said to Dal that I wanted to take him out for dinner tonight and, in a gesture of goodwill, I told him to ask his mother if she wanted to come too. I really did not expect her to want to see me since our divorce of seven years had not been all that pleasant for either of us, especially her. I had remarried four years ago, but we had not even seen each other in five years, and only spoken twice. Correspondence had been mainly about money: how I should have been more successful, made more money, given her more money, and on and on. I always felt that she should have been willing and able to get established financially herself, either with teaching or some other work, but she always felt as if I should provide for her regardless. Such was the background to the differences of opinion as we met again at the Old Country Buffet in Roanoke. Dal had invited his mother, and much to my surprise, she accepted. Even more to my surprise, however, we had a very pleasant evening. The conversation was all sweetness and light, with no attempts to solve all the problems of the world tonight, especially with our son there. I was sincerely pleased that the dinner went so well and that there was no bitterness resurrected. As we started to leave the restaurant, Jean surprised me again by saying that she had not seen Peppy in a long time, probably would not get another chance in his lifetime since he was nine years old now, and could she and Dal come back to my campground? I was happy to accommodate them and it gave me an opportunity to give my other son his first ride on a GoldWing, all the way back to the Dixie Caverns Campground in Salem, about 8 or 9 miles south of Tanglewood Square where we ate. I stopped after a few miles to give Dal my winter riding gauntlet gloves since his hands were freezing in the cool October evening wind. He may have enjoyed the ride as much as Ray, but he did not express any feelings to me. I think the ride itself, leaning into curves, being out in the open at 50 miles an hour, and the rapid acceleration of the bike (even with two "fat asses" on it), tended to scare him somewhat.

Once again Pep went through his routine of jumps and hoops at seeing another family member for the first time in many years. I didn't expect him to remember everyone after so long, but if he was at all confused about who Jean was, he surely did not show it. We threw his Frisbee around for about half an hour until it started to get dark. Dal reminded me, once again, that he was in bad need of a new VCR. So I told him that Sandy and I had decided to give him one for his birthday and Christmas combined. He then put in a further request for his favorite brand, just to make sure it was fully compatible with their TV and remote control, etc. There really wasn't much else to talk about on the totally non-essential, no conflict level, so I finally told them I was ready to turn in for the night. They bid me farewell and were gone into the darkness. As I drifted to sleep, I was grateful the evening had gone so well and that we all had enjoyed the visit.

Fran, Jason, and Mr. Beam

Dal and the "Rambler".

Day 21: MORE VIRGINIA

This was going to be another short day in terms of distance; I was riding only to Charlottesville where my daughter lives, about 120 miles away. Since our plan was not to meet until she got off from work at 3 p.m., I had some spare time this morning to do a little sight-seeing. Although I had lived in Roanoke for over three years, I had never taken a tour of the "famous" Dixie Caverns, the tourist attraction touted at this campsite where I was staying. In fact, I have not been a real big fan of wandering around inside caves since I was a kid but this seemed like a good time to renew that adventuresome activity.

I ambled over to the country store where they sold tickets and signed up for the 9 a.m. tour, starting in half an hour. The lady behind the counter was right in tune with my own heart. When she saw on my registration that I was from Colorado, she sighed that she had lived in Longmont for a number of years and couldn't wait to get back. "Just out of curiosity, what exactly is it you find most different?", I asked, thinking she was going to say either the weather or the scenery. Instead, she responded "I like the way people out west say what they think. Here, everyone just nods and smiles, and you never know what's really on their mind. Even worse, they say 'Come see us' when they hope you never cross their door step again. I'm sick and tired of having to be a damn mind reader to get along with people in the South." I could hardly contain my enthusiastic agreement for every sentiment she expressed and told her so. I was just dumfounded that someone else felt so strongly against what my ex-mother-in-law called "social manners." I have been in many uncomfortable situations where the only way to have known how someone really felt was to have been a "damn mind reader," not my strong suit either. Since this lady was obviously not one to hold back her opinions, I asked if the caverns were worth seeing, and with the same candor she said, "yes, but only once."

The tour started right on time, all three of us and the tour guide. Instead of going *down* to the caves, we actually climbed *up* into the mountain to the "cathedral room." Other "rooms" had names such as "Turkey Wing," "Wedding Bell," and "Magic Mirror," and all had the same damp, drippy atmosphere, but were interesting nonetheless. At one point, the guide said that the stalactites were still living, growing organisms which are very sensitive to outside contaminants, including oil on human skin, and odors or germs on your clothing. "At one cavern in New Mexico," she continued, "they make you take off your clothes before they let you go in to the cavern." A southern teenager, on the tour with her mother, exclaimed, "You mean strip down nekkid?" The guide said she didn't know for sure since she had never been there, "It could be they give you a gown or something clean and sterile to wear." Whatever, they were not going to get that fifteen-year-old to walk around with no clothes on!

After the tour, I went back to the campsite to take Pep for a little walk before we headed north to Charlottesville. A man and his wife were hooking their

Ford Explorer up to the back of what had to be the biggest RV I had ever seen in my life. Not only was it long, it was wide and expensive-looking. On top, where there usually is nothing, a satellite dish was perched with hydraulic arms to raise, lower and rotate the dish, for perfect reception no matter where they were parked. I tried to be somewhat reserved, but I couldn't help myself as I gushed "Boy, that is the biggest camper I've ever seen. You must do a lot of traveling."

"Yes," he said, "We used to live near Austin, Texas when I was working, but now, we just go where we feel like going, and live in this year round."

"You mean you don't have a home anymore?" I inquired.

"That's right. We have a pad near Palm Springs, California, we own, but they rent it out when we're not there, which is most of the time." We talked some more and he told me, with more than a little bit of pride, that he had almost $250 thousand dollars invested in his rig, more than a lot of people have in their homes, and that he and his wife enjoy traveling. They have children and grandchildren all over the country and plan to see all of them once a year. "When we get tired, we just stay in one place for a while." His Holiday Rambler Imperial more closely resembled a Trailways bus than an RV. It was 38 feet long, had a Cummins Diesel engine, a 6 speed automatic transmission, and as smooth a ride as anything on the road. He was going to give me a tour inside, but his wife confessed to having something not in perfect order and asked if she could give me a rain check until later this morning. I thanked them both for the offer and hospitality, but I wanted to get on down the road. I will never forget that conversation, though, particularly the part about not even having a home anymore. It seems so abnormal until you think about it: retired, comfortable income, good health, lots of family and relatives all over the country, and most importantly, that's what they *both* want to do. Yes, why not indeed?

With that little bit of sightseeing and wanderlust over, I whistled for Pep and we were off for Charlottesville. It was not yet noon and the trip usually took two hours so we had plenty of time to meet our 3 p.m. date with Fran, my daughter. I decided to take the leisurely exit route out of Roanoke, and visited some old stomping grounds. Our former house on Bobwhite Lane was still the same off white color it had been seven years ago. The neighborhood was definitely middle class with lots of bicycles and minivans everywhere. Although I was happy to see my old house again, I had no desire to roll back the clock. Our unhappy marriage, a failed business partnership, and the provincial nature of Virginia in general made me proud to tell everyone I was from Colorado. It's a state that bespeaks the "New West." Virginia, on the other hand, represents the "Old South," a legacy of which I had more than my share the last 20 years. I rode up Williamson Road, a major north-south business artery in Roanoke, and saw my old company. The new president had let the exterior deteriorate both in appearance and product signage. I felt, for the first time since I left in 1988, a sense of relief at not being associated with a small office equipment dealership. If I were still the president of that company, I realized, I could not be taking a six week cross country motorcycle adventure, something I'm enjoying more than any other endeavor in my whole life. Also, the very idea of being responsible for 36 employees, and their payroll, while once an exciting challenge to me, now seemed like a giant pain in the backside. I was so relieved that no employee, or their spouse, was calling to complain about the health insurance plan, or the vacation schedule, or the "better offer" they had from a competitor. I am now a writer whose job is to entertain and inform my readers, and in so doing, find my reward. Perhaps that will be less than a small business owner makes, maybe not. In any case, I am so happy doing what I am doing that the money is of little consequence. Too late have I learned that doing what you enjoy is more rewarding than reaping a huge income. (Of course, next year, if I'm on welfare, I reserve the right to revise my opinion!)

The ride up Interstate 81 that afternoon was simply sublime. Light, warm air, fall colors everywhere on the oak, maple, and hickory trees, and a joyful spirit to match. Nobody from the University of Virginia Alumnae Association asked my net worth as I pulled into Charlottesville that afternoon, but I surely would have confounded them with my statement of wealth. They just don't measure it the same way I do. They probably would have disowned me anyway for being on a motorcycle and all. "Sort of stuffy" is a way most folks describe the University, and with good reason. The fact that "Mr. Jefferson" founded the University in 1819 has carried over to this day. Many faculty members and alumnae administrators speak as if they just had lunch with him, and they speak with all the authority and blessing of the "Sage of Monticello." It's almost a religious sanctimoniousness, something I have more disdain for as I get older, not less.

My daughter was only a few minutes late when I met her outside the Sheraton Hotel off Route 29 north.

Pep did his usual flips for a long-lost relative, and we walked around the hotel grounds for a brief period of salutation, more Pep than I. Fran was now living with her boyfriend at his parents' home and I had planned to camp out in their driveway for one night if that was okay with the parents, whom I had never met. Fran had a 1988 Ford Taurus which my wife and I had bought for her when she graduated from college a couple of years earlier. I was pleasantly surprised that she had taken such good care of the automobile, and honestly, it looked as good as when we gave it to her. She asked me to follow her out to the Ward family compound in Crozet which I agreed to do. Then, at near-dangerous and certainly illegal speeds, she threaded her way around back roads I had not been on in at least 20 years, if ever. Like Ray, her idea of a compliment was "Not bad, Dad, I didn't think you could keep up with me."

"Thanks a lot, Fran; I'm glad I foiled your attempt to lose me," I said while pretending contempt. "You didn't think I was going to be riding a *slow* motorcycle, did you?" She laughed with that same glee she has had all her life when she thinks she has gotten away with mischief, and I mimicked a prize fighter ready to punch her out.

First the mother, Wanda, then the boyfriend, Jason, and finally the father, Billy, all came home to the farm for our evening social gathering. I was offered a bathroom with shower if I wanted to "clean up." I gladly made use of the facilities in their new house, built on the family farmstead and within eyesight of the house where Billy was born and raised. *His* parents had also built a new house, on the other side of the original dwelling, which had fallen into disrepair amidst towering oak trees.

I had agreed to take Fran and Jason out to dinner, and I hoped that Billy and Wanda would also join us, but they declined. Then I called Sandy at home in Colorado before we left for the restaurant so everybody was all up to date on my progress, especially with family and ex-relatives. When I told my wife I had a very pleasant meeting last night with my ex-wife, she asked, "Well, did you kiss and make up?"

"No! It wasn't *that* pleasant," I shreeked. They have never met each other, but everyone who knows both, including my parents and children, say the two women's personalities are like night and day. I guess that is good. I would be the last one to want to repeat my same mistakes, over and over, if I had a choice.

Fran and Jason had a place all picked out for dinner, Awful Arthur's, which didn't sound that great to me, but I was relieved they had not set their pitter pattering hearts on the Boar's Head Inn, because that restaurant would have broken the piggy bank for the rest of my trip. I've heard of dinner there costing $100 per person with fine wine from "Mr. Jefferson's" vineyard, no less. Jason drove us to Awful Arthur's where we also had some good wine, along with some excellent seafood. Unfortunately, Billy had poured a Jim Beam highball down my throat before we went out to eat, thus causing a predictable aftermath: I had a terrible hangover the next morning as I slept in while almost everyone else in the family got up to go to work.

For the first time on this entire trip, Pep was *inside* the tent-camper with me. Billy Ward has a pack of six or eight Beagle hounds with the most sensitive and active noses to be found on any dog anywhere.

When they smelled another canine, after Jason let them out of the shed where they had spent the night, they immediately started whinning they were so excited about being on a new scent. I peered out of my tent as they raced around in circles, ending up right at my zippered flap, pink and black noses twitching in the air. Pep and I both stared at them as the whole pack proceeded to bark and howl up a storm, just as if they had a raccoon in a tree. It would have been even funnier if I had not had such a bad headache from over indulgence the night before. Finally, another family member came out and put the dogs back in the garage where they could only sniff through a two inch crack, but could not reach Pep or me. Once again, we had worn out our welcome, and it was time to move on to the Blue Ridge Parkway and another gorgeous fall day.

Day 22: The SKYLINE DRIVE

Leaving Albemarle County, Virginia that October morning was another excuse to become permanently addicted to this type of motorcycle touring. Perfectly calm air, with bright sunshine sparkling over nature's boldest colorings of trees and shrubs, painted a background for horses and cattle grazing in the green fields of alfalfa and clover. If there ever was a time to see the Piedmont section of Virginia, this was it. The U.Va. Alumnae Association boasts that every year, when the football games draw old graduates back to Charlottesville, the real estate brokers sell farms and estates, some costing millions, to alumnae who had no intention of buying any property during their class reunions. I can understand why, with the attraction of an academic village, coupled with rolling hills in spectacular foliage, and pleasant memories of years gone by.

Speaking from my experience, however, owning a 200 year old house and farm, while charming in character and history, also involves a lot more work and inconvenience than I ever anticipated when I signed on the dotted line in 1967. Emotional decisions are usually not rational ones, something I am still trying to learn.

Route 250 west from Crozet goes right up Afton Mountain to Waynesboro, the entrance to the Blue Ridge Parkway and Skyline Drive. Although the Blue Ridge Parkway continues south to North Carolina, the Skyline Drive portion is most famous for its spectacular mountain beauty as it winds its way north to Front Royal, Virginia, 72 miles west of Washington,D.C. The Appalachian Trail runs parallel to both the Blue Ridge Parkway for 469 miles, and the Skyline Drive for 106 miles, through Virginia and North Carolina. The Shenandoah National Park, established by Congress in 1926, totally surrounds the Skyline Drive portion, and the National Park Service administers both areas. Any other road is faster than the Skyline Drive with a speed limit of 35 m.p.h., but nothing is more beautiful on a fall day. The park literature states that foliage color peaks between October 10th and 25th. I had the privilege of riding on Saturday, October 16th, a perfectly clear day.

    Since I had not yet had any breakfast, the Howard Johnson restaurant in Waynesboro was a welcomed stop. While I was inside enjoying some ham and eggs, a rather loud group of men, some in leathers and chaps, came in and the hostess seated them only a few tables away from mine. I put up with their boisterous stories and jokes until I was leaving the restaurant. There, in the parking lot on the other side of my bike and trailer, about 5 or 6 motorcycles were parked, and 4 of them were GoldWings! I immediately went back inside to visit with these guys who suddenly were more like gentlemen than I had previously supposed. One of the younger riders was totally amazed that I had ridden across the country with my dog and camper. He seemed genuinely interested so I gave him one of our souvenir photos in front of the Rocky Mountains, creating a certain envy among his co-riders. They were all going up the Skyline Drive for a Saturday ride, about 200 miles altogether. We had a few more laughs, and then I said good-bye since I had hoped to get up to Washington, D.C. by nightfall, and the parkway beckoned.

Rockfish Gap is an elevation of just under 2,000 feet. We would climb over the next 55 miles to the Upper Hawksbill Overlook at 3,630 feet, a little below the peak of 4,051 and the highest point in the Shenandoah National Park. All along the drive are pull offs for scenic views and opportunities to take photographs. The Moorman's River Overlook and Wildcat Ridge lead to Loft Mountain, a full service area in the park offering not only a restaurant, but also camp and trailer sites, gasoline, gift shops and nature trails. I would have enjoyed staying there, but the timing was not right on this particular day. We continued on to the Skyland area, which at 3,680 feet elevation, is the highest point on the Drive and also a primary tourist facility. Naturalist George Freeman Pollack built the Skyland Resort in the 1890's and was a major proponent for establishing the park, which was completed before his death. The riding horse stables are said to be located in the same place he had originally laid out for his own resort guests at the turn of the century. I especially enjoyed having lunch there and being able to watch other tourists come up to Peppy who was tied up outside, just begging for attention (or food) from any sympathetic passersby.

When I went out to unhook him after my sandwich, a gal with an Australian Shepherd stopped to see if Pep was the same breed. They looked about the same size but her dog had a cropped tail, only 2 inches long. We let the dogs romp around for a short run, and she offered to watch Pep while I went into the gift shop to buy some Virginia wine for my Aunt Lil in

Pennsylvania, with whom I would be staying tomorrow night. Dog lovers have a common bond of their affection for animals in general and their own breed in particular. Although Pep was not an Australian Shepherd, the breeds are very close and I'm sure both dogs enjoyed the camaraderie. I thanked her for the pooch sitting, without ever asking her name, and we were on our way again up the Parkway to Thornton Gap.

The smooth road surface, with continual switchbacks on gradual curves, provided a good test for a cyclist's ability to establish a rhythm in turns, which is very pleasing to the senses. I was apprehensive about only one hazard: the fallen leaves. Since it was well into fall, the trees had been dropping leaves for several weeks, and in places where the highway had been wet, they seemed to stick to the road in a dangerous, slippery way. I did not "push" any turns with leaves on the ground and kept the same vigilance as I would with snow or sand. When we finally reached Thornton Gap, as scenic as the Skyline Drive had been, I was ready to turn east to Sperryville on Route 211, a regular, and straighter, state highway.

Another 55 miles put us in Manassas, Virginia, only 18 miles from Washington, D.C. I looked for a campground and found the Hillwood RV Park, a combination of RV storage, camp ground and trailer park, plus the homestead's original farmhouse. The owner/manager was a sort of dry businessman who went out of his way to avoid even the appearance of having a sense of humor. For a semi-excuse, he confessed to having bought some additional property in 1987, as an investment, just before the real estate market collapsed. He said he might not live long

The Skyline Drive

enough to get his money back out of that "strip mall on Route 29," like I was supposed to feel sorry for him or something. "It's worth only half of what I paid for it right now, after 5 years." I tried to cheer him up a little with my story of our trip, which he asked about after seeing the Colorado vehicle registration, but for the first time in over 30 states, he declined to keep the souvenir photograph. "Don't want to be obligated to you," he said, "might have to kick you out later if you or the dog cause any problems for the other campers."

"Well I certainly hope it doesn't come to that," I said. "We haven't been asked to leave any other place yet," not that I could immediately recall, anyway. His gruffness bothered me the more I thought about it as we made our way back to the tent area, way around back of the sales area, the storage area, the pool and tennis court, the banquet hall, and row after row of RV campsites on concrete pads. This was probably the biggest campground trailer operation I had seen on the entire trip, and the grumpiest manager/owner. I used to tell my new salespeople, when they started their training by making cold calls on offices, that neither they nor I could be responsible for unusual, discourteous, or just plain rude behavior on the part of other people. "You never know whether a check bounced from the bank, the baby has diarrhea, or their love life isn't what it should be, and they are surely not going to tell you," I would say, "so just chalk it up to something wrong with *them* and go on to the next person." I tried to follow my own advice as I set up camp and fed Pep. Sure enough, when I went over to the restroom facilities area to use the pay phone to call home, there was an entirely different group of poorer and friendlier folk. One old guy who hardly had said "Hello" to me asked if I knew what town we were in. When I told him I thought it was Manassas, he said "That's right and do you know what happened here?"

Somehow, by the way the other people were snickering, I knew he wasn't talking about the Battle of Bull Run so I said, "Do you mean Lorena Bobbit and all that?"

"Yea," he said, "this is Manassas, where women are real women..., and men sleep on their stomachs. Ha,ha,ha."

He enjoyed his own humor so much it was hard not to laugh along with him, as did the other two women and another man. They had an open bottle of Wild Turkey on a card table set up on the porch to lubricate their senses of humor. "You're welcome to have a drink with us..., if you know any good stories," the old fellow said as he extended a slightly used paper cup.

I politely declined since I honestly was more interested in finding a place to eat dinner than I was in having a drink under those congenial but unsanitary conditions. When I got back from dinner, I used the phone in a much quieter atmosphere, either because the booze was all gone or they had just gotten sleepy and went back to their trailers. It was ironic, I thought, that the manager had threatened to throw Pep and me out for being a disturbance when this rowdiness was being carried on by the regulars. No matter, we had a great night's sleep and didn't hear another peep until morning.`

On top of Ol' Smokie.

Cruisin' the Skyline Drive.

Day 23: WASHINGTON, D.C., MARYLAND & DELAWARE

Fortunately for my disposition this Sunday morning, I didn't see the manager again. Pep and I went for a stimulating walk down a wooded trail going from the tent area through some heavy hardwood forest to the main highway. It was obvious, even on the weekend, that we were near a major metropolis with all the traffic and construction activity. Concrete trucks strained their diesel engines as they hauled material to another building site, oblivious to the Sabbath. We had a panoramic view from this little hilltop over looking the Lee Highway as Route 29 is known here. What used to be a peaceful suburb was being transformed into Washington sprawl with office buildings, shopping centers, and other developments. The Metro Line had extended the commuter train to a new station only a few miles from here, near the Beltway, thereby assuring a constant flow of people and vehicles as long as the Federal Government continues to operate. This is Fairfax County, Virginia, a boom and bustle community if ever there was one, in spite of the Hillwood campground owner's lament about his mall site. For some reason, I had a strange feeling of omnipotence as Pep and I watched everyone below us struggling to compete in their economic life. Pep could take only so much of this philosophic activity, however, especially when he heard some rustling in the trees and leaves behind us. It had to be a squirrel! The heck with the economy, he was ready to give chase to another Virginia varmint, and so he did. We then made it back to the tent area without any further excitement and were on our way to the nation's capital by 8 a.m.

The Lee Highway merged into Arlington Boulevard which became Route 50 and then Wilson Boulevard in Arlington, Virginia. The office buildings here were in the process of being torn down to make way for new, bigger, and, of course, more expensive buildings of the same genre. I remembered one of the old ones as we passed by; it was where I had my first employment interview with Xerox Corporation in 1967. For some reason, they offered me a job and that was the beginning of a 15 year career, off and on, in the office machines business. I thought the business had peaked out and left them after a short stint, but they managed to struggle along without me! A wiser man than I once said, on leaving a big corporation, "you are missed about as long as it takes for water to fill in the hole when you pull your finger out." It's true. When you're gone, no matter how good or bad a job you might have done, nothing stops, someone else merely picks up where you left off and everything rolls along. Nature may abhor a vacuum, but so do big corporations.

We crossed the Potomac River on the Arlington Memorial Bridge and continued east on Constitution Avenue. We passed the Lincoln Memorial, the Vietnam Memorial, the Washington Monument. Then, on the north side, stood the White House, poised with dignity befitting a head of state. Constitution Avenue merged with Pennsylvania Avenue right in front of the U.S. Capitol and we then turned south on New Jersey Avenue to stop at the marina on the Potomac River.

After a short walk, I decided I wanted to keep moving because some of the characters drifting around didn't look like they had any good intentions. An older man and his wife, however, gave me rough directions to New York Avenue which they said would lead to Maryland, our next goal.

Somewhere around Florida Avenue and 18th street, I knew that regardless of whether I was following the directions correctly or not, I was in trouble. The stop light had just turned red, but off to my right, on a corner of the intersection, were about 10 or 12 kids, teenagers and juvenile delinquents, some black, some white, and some Asian, all loitering around with a boom box so loud it blasted the whole neighborhood. But what bothered me the most was the way they were all pretending to fight with each other, sort of slapping and kicking at the same time. One of the ring leaders had a Mohawk hairdo, with the top part dyed a pink and purple combination. Several had brass or gold earrings dangling on the side of sinister faces. When "tough guy" looked over at me and my rig, and then back at his buddies, I didn't care if the traffic light was red, green, or yellow, I looked for a break in the line of cars, and I was out of there, fast. They yelled epithets and lunged at me as I accelerated, with only a fleeting glance back. If a cop pulled me over, I would have been happy to plead my case of fear and more fear, at least he would have provided some armed protection from the local hoodlums. For the first time in my whole journey, I was genuinely afraid of being robbed or mugged. The look that the weirdo gave me was no ordinary glance; it was a sizing up of a mischief opportunity, and I did not want to be the object of their attention. I had a small pistol in my tank bag, which I knew was illegal, but they probably had guns too, and I did not want to be involved in a shoot-out. How could this be happening only a few blocks from the Capitol? I rode ahead to Bladensburg Road, which was supposed to intersect with Highway 50 again, and if my map was right, that would take us to Annapolis and the Chesapeake Bay Bridge. I didn't stop until we got to the Naval Academy, and then only to walk around a little and reflect on my close call. I will never forget the feeling of helplessness and vulnerability at that intersection in Washington,D.C. The boys were totally bored, nothing to do with their time or their energies, and I just happened to ride up next to them, an opportunity for excitement and conquest, all rolled into one motorcycle ridden by a middle-aged man with his dog in a cage behind him. I will not live long enough to ever go back to downtown Washington,D.C. on a motorcycle by myself. I would want at a least 5 or 6 bikes before being confronted by that gang again, and even then, I'd just as soon bypass the whole event. It's not a battle I want to wage, and I now understand how many people in big cities feel when they say they are afraid of the growing threat, and reality, of crime. I'd move too, and I did.

The Bay Bridge provided an awesome view of the Chesapeake Bay. It may be only a tributary of water, but to me, it looked like the ocean itself. Whenever I cannot see the shore on either side, it might just as well be the ocean. It's a body of water that seems to go on forever, even though we were on a bridge which I knew, in my heart of hearts, had to find land on the other side - at some point! Unlike the Mississippi River which had a gentle flow to the navigation, these tugs and barges were struggling against waves and wind as they forged ahead with their cargoes, covered by tarpaulins of canvas.

Route 301 continued up the eastern shore of Maryland for another 50 miles before the great state of Delaware welcomed us to its borders. All signs north pointed to Wilmington, and we were there in what seemed to be no time at all. This was definitely not Montana! Flat straight roads, of good repair, made for easy traveling as I stopped to call my Aunt Lil in Mechanicsville, Pennsylvania with an estimated time of arrival. As always, she bubbled over with enthusiasm at the prospect of seeing me again, the first time in a lot of years.

My father was born in Budapest, Hungary, in 1898, the oldest of what was to be eleven children, my Aunt Lil one of the youngest. Their father emigrated to America around the turn of the century to seek a sense of freedom and fortune which eluded a tailor in the old country, both Germany and Hungary. When Grandfather Schmalz had established himself and his trade in Buffalo, New York, he sent for my grandmother and father who came over to join him. Although it sounds strange now, my father wanted to continue in high school but my grandfather thought so much schooling was useless for a young man, and the really valuable pursuit was to learn a trade, something you could do with your hands, like being a tailor. The high school principal in Buffalo, a Mr. Stagg, apparently felt my father had intellectual promise and offered for Dad to live with him so that he would not be a burden on the Schmalz family which needed everyone to carry their own weight and the older children helped out with the younger ones, who were being born with clock-like regularity. My father did well enough in high school to be offered a scholarship at Princeton University where he also completed a Masters Degree program in Economics. Later, he would write several books and newsletters on the economy, thick with his forecasts and fiscal appraisals. World history was also evolving rapidly at this time leading to my father joining the American troops in the First World War. Anti-German sentiments were so strong in this country, however, that he decided to legally change his name from "Schmalz" to "Lawrence," an acceptable English sounding name. Some of his siblings followed his example, and also changed their names to Lawrence, while others retained the Schmalz family name. My Uncle Ed, who died last year and left the inheritance for my brothers and me, mentioned previously, was named Edwin Schmalz. My father died in 1950, when I was only six years old, and he was only 52, so everything I know about his family has been passed down over the years. My recollections may not be entirely accurate, with all deference to those of his siblings still alive.

My earliest memories of my Aunt Lil, who by now was wondering how I had gotten lost, were of warm and busy gatherings at this same farmhouse in Bucks County Pennsylvania. I have a lot of relatives who know how to cook, some better than others, but nobody can hold a candle to this wonderful lady when it comes to putting out a mammoth spread of food. I have seen her, on more than one occasion, prepare a six or seven course dinner for a dozen people, seated at 2 or 3 tables, all the while carrying on light and pleasant conversations with everyone at the same time! Just like there was nothing to it. As good as the food, though, was the warmth and hospitality of her home. She was always cheerful and smiling with plenty of hugs and kisses for all. So now at her 81 years of age, should I expect anything different? Not a chance. Even though I was late getting there, she had the same warm and friendly manner which she has had since I can remember from my earliest childhood, a long way back to be sure. I loved visiting with her again that night, hearing about how different members of my father's family were doing, and in due course, being told of those who had passed on. We drifted back and forth from past to present, and back again, all in the course of an hour or two. Pep enjoyed the chicken scraps after we had finished eating, and we both slept in the same room my uncle had occupied before his death. A sense of history and harmony filled my mind as I went to bed that night, grateful for my family in all its diverse history and branches.

A little town in New Jersey
(that New York hasn't touched).

Time for a dip!

Day 24: NEW JERSEY

Breakfast at Aunt Lil's was almost as good as dinner the night before. I was feeling more rested, and we picked up the family ties right where we had left off. Her son Joey, who lives and works in another part of the farmstead, came over for a brief visit as I showed them both the motorcycle and camper rig in the daylight. I could have stayed longer and enjoyed every minute of it, but I had promised my younger brother, Guy, who lives in Connecticut, that we would be there by late afternoon and I did not know the way. Also, I had called the Minolta Corporate Headquarters in Ramsey, New Jersey to see if I could get my camera fixed on the way to New England, and they had agreed to try.

The sunshine was out in full force now showing off the aged colonial beauty of this part of Pennsylvania. It had been so long since I had driven through Bucks County, I truly had forgotten how quaint and charming this part of the country was. Almost every house had a stone wall around the front entrance and many had horses grazing in adjacent fields, criss-crossed with split-rail fencing. The old houses were full of character and, much to the credit of the architectural zoning committees, the new homes blended in with the old in a most appealing mixture. A few miles up Pennsylvania Route 202 to New Hope, and we were crossing the Delaware River, the border with New Jersey. These states in the Northeast are a fraction the size of Montana, or God forbid, Texas. Instead of taking 3 days to cross a state, I was moving through 3 states in one day! Granted, I had not gone from one end of each to the other, but there were still huge differences in geography that are more apparent in the wind than on a map.

Route 202 in New Jersey was a continuation of the same road from Pennsylvania, cutting a northeast diagonal across the state. The first part was more picturesque, and a lot less populated. By the time we reached Bridgewater, about the upper third of the state, it was painfully obvious that this part of New Jersey was a suburb of New York City. All roads became jammed with harried drivers, each one in more of a hurry than the vehicle ahead of him, and a cacophony of horns made the image complete. More construction, louder horns, and many more trucks were the norm as we went through Parsipanny and points north. Then, as suddenly as it had overwhelmed us, the commercial activity subsided as we entered Ramsey and Upper Saddle River, New Jersey.

My visit to Minolta Corporate headquarters was a very satisfying one. The camera Customer Service Department, realizing that I did not have 2 weeks to wait for a normal repair turnaround time, asked me to go to lunch while they worked on diagnosing and repairing my Maxxum problem. I had the distinct feeling that if they were not able to fix it, they would have given me a new one rather than have me spend the rest of my trip, and my time writing this book, without a Minolta camera I had paid several hundred dollars to buy only a year ago. Fortunately, there was some defect which they said had occurred during the manufacturing process, had nothing to do with my handling of the camera, and they were able to repair it perfectly and permanently in their lab right there. I was overjoyed to be "shooting" again and took some pictures of the majestic Minolta Corporate Park just to test the repairs before I left.

Now, I was on my way to Connecticut and traveling east over the Hudson River on the absolutely spectacular Bear Mountain Bridge. Looking north was Ossining, Croton-on-Hudson, and beyond that, the U.S. Military Academy at West Point. To the south, the Hudson flowed past Dobbs Ferry and Englewood Cliffs to Manhattan, all shrouded with the brilliant fall colors of thousands of hardwood trees growing on the river's edge. I had to stop and gawk, now on the New York side, in addition to taking some memorable scenic photographs with my newly reconditioned camera.

Incredible as it may seem, New York state, at this most narrow distance, is only 12 miles from the Connecticut line. Actually, I ended up crossing *back* into New York on my way to the Ridgefield turnoff. And Guy's house is within walking distance of the state line, he said.

The town of Ridgefield is a typical southern New England village: founded in the early 1700s, a central main street which has several historical buildings, huge oak and maple trees line the sidewalks, and a general air of prosperity as evidenced by the abundance of Volvo station wagons and Mercedes sedans. I stopped to buy some wine as a host gift for my brother and also to get some directions to his house on curvy back roads. Everyone in the wine store knew of the fine dining establishment near Guy's house, O'Bair's Maxine restaurant, and pointed me in the right direction. The store manager said he knew where it was, even if he could not afford to eat there, "a most expensive place, even for this town." I had been to his house a year ago, but I was following Guy that time so I really did not remember every turn as we made our way into the countryside. Several horse farms looked familiar across the road as I turned onto a steeply-slopping gravel driveway I thought was Guy's. Part way up the hill, however, two enormous German Shepherd dogs came bounding out of the woods to greet me and I knew I had the wrong driveway. With no room to turn around and no desire to violate these guard dogs' territory any more than I already had, I gripped the front hand brake and put down both feet to keep the bike from tipping over as I started to slide backwards down the gravel road. The incline was so steep that the front brake by itself would not hold both the bike and the trailer on the loose gravel. I tried my best to keep the rig straight up as we slid back down toward the main road. Once, feeling that I was off balance and going to go down, I released the brake and slowly accelerated forward. With the rear wheel spinning slightly, I started back up the hill again, only to have "Fang and Killer" come charging back over, frothing at the mouth and ready to attack. On with the brake again, slide backwards down the hill, try not to jack-knife or fall over, feet apart for balance and stabilizers, we finally made it to the bottom. I looked up the hill at my two tormentors who had stopped barking but were all eyes on me and Pep. In my most stern, deep-voiced command, I yelled, "Bad dog! Shame! Shame!" They both put their tails between their legs and slunk away toward friendlier masters as I awkwardly turned around to continue down the lane.

  I finally found the right driveway, there are no names, but Guy's house was even more beautiful than I had remembered it, and his hospitality made all my trials and tribulations worthwhile. He had acquired a Cocker Spaniel named "Max," a blonde, wavy-furred critter who, after a few preliminary sniffs, decided Pep and I were okay for a visit. In no time at all, the two dogs were both chasing sticks and play toys through giant piles of leaves and made every appearance of having been buddies for a long time, a much more pleasant reception than we almost got from the attack pack next door. Fully worn out after lots of running and romping, and I well-fed after wining and dining with my brother, Pep and I once again retired for the night to the guest bedroom. This was no ordinary room, but by far the most opulent guest room either of us had experienced on this trip - marble bathroom fixtures, decorator designed bedspreads and curtains, which blended in with the wallpaper, etc. We both tried to pretend it was normal and cleaned up our act a notch or two so as not to offend the good taste of our host. I could tell Pep was impressed as he curled up on a Persian rug next to my bed. In a matter of minutes, however, those tell-tale shimmies and shakes of his feet, plus a few whimpers, indicated he had started chasing rabbits in his dreams, or perhaps, "Fang and Killer" were chasing him, I'm never sure which.

Senic Susquehanna River

Bear Mountain Suspension Bridge

Day 25: CONNECTICUT

My younger brother and I had a great visit over breakfast the next morning. We talked about our family, business and financial problems, and what options were open to everyone involved. Guy had been a very successful executive with a large commercial real estate development firm in New York City, but that market had taken a terrible downturn in the last year, and he was now on his own. After almost 20 years in the same industry, however, he had so many business contacts and associates that the possibilities for new projects or deals always seem to be present. Just the two of us, together in his house for that one day and one night visit, plus the clowning around of our dogs, was probably the best time I can remember sharing with my younger brother. Even though I was 49 and he was 45, we really had not spent much time together growing up, always away at different schools, or starting careers in distant places. I was grateful for the opportunity to get to know my own brother better than I ever had in the past, and I think he appreciated the camaraderie, too.

We left Guy's house at about 10 a.m., on another gorgeous fall day, although this would soon end. The color was definitely past the peak at this point in Connecticut, however, and leaves were piled up everywhere or drifting around from gentle breezes.

Unlike the stone walls in Bucks County, Pennsylvania, the rocks here climbed steeper terrain with gently-rolling hills becoming not so smooth anymore. Even with the leaves falling, it was difficult to see long distances because the land was more rugged. There are no straight roads, except for the interstates, in this part of southern New England. Although I had grown up in Old Greenwich, Connecticut, not many miles from Ridgefield, I was seeing a new state for the first time as we rode toward Danbury. Oh I had been on this very road, Route 7, years ago with my parents as we drove to my boarding school in Lakeville, but that was simply not the same as today. On a touring motorcycle, with the wind in my face and sunshine on my back, my dog and camper behind me, I was once again feeling just as I had in Yellowstone several weeks ago: the luckiest guy on earth to be able to have this unparalleled freedom to roam and explore the same country I had been in earlier, but without the constraints of time, money, youth, or business obligations.

    I pulled off on a hill overlooking Danbury and took a little time to contemplate the city, which used to be famous for the production of hats, but now had a diversified manufacturing and industrial base. All of Connecticut appears to be basically well off, as it should with the highest family income in the country, $49,199. The streets are in good repair, town parks and civic centers are scattered everywhere, and, of course, those ubiquitous signs telling travelers when the city was founded. In Danbury's case, the town was settled in 1685 and incorporated in 1702. But I was surprised to read that the Danbury Fair, so famous and popular when I was a kid, had been discontinued in 1981. Connecticut residents must have too much money to be involved with, or interested in, agriculture and related fair activities.

From Danbury, I could have stayed on Interstate 84 all the way to Hartford, but I chose the slower and more interesting Route 202. This scenic road took us from village to village, through New Milford, Litchfield, Torrington, Avon, and finally, into Hartford. We stopped for lunch outside of Avon, Connecticut only 8 miles east of Hartford, the state capital and "insurance center" for the country with 35 headquarters located here. Riding into the city from the east, on a state highway and not an interstate, I saw what was probably the poorest section in all of the state. Many Latin American and Caribbean communities made their homes along this road, as evidenced by their store names and culturally distinct dress. Many groups of people were congregating on street corners and open air markets, but I never had any feeling of danger as I had in Washington,D.C. Not even close to the same apprehension because these ethnic groups had their own activities and productive interaction, buying and selling of goods and services, not just loitering around looking for trouble. Hardly anyone paid attention to us as we slowly rode from one section of town to another, even though it was obvious I was not a native resident.

Colt Park, originally the estate of the Colt revolver inventor, was an interesting historical diversion. Once again, however, all Pep cared about was sniffing the trunks of those big oak trees in an attempt to figure out where the squirrels had gone. He just knew they were up there, but he could not climb a tree, much to his disappointment and the squirrel's delight. They chattered like crazy, hopping from limb to limb right in front of him as he barked and yipped in frustration. "Why won't they come down and play with you?" I asked in jest. A vigorous jumping with a quick series of short barks was his reply, much to the amusement of other tourists and passersby. "Okay, we'll just have to get them another time," I said. "Let's go," and he immediately ran over to his kennel, not to be left behind, even for a chase with the squirrels.

We crossed the Connecticut River into the eastern part of the state just as afternoon clouds were beginning to form. The wind also picked up, and it started to rain when we entered Rhode Island an hour later. No problem, I thought, I'll just put on my trusty rain gear and wait for the bad weather to blow over. Chepachet, Rhode Island was another 6 or 7 miles down Route 44, but by now it was a steady drizzle. I stopped at small service station- restaurant combination, had a cup of coffee, and got the local weather *advice*. The cook and maitre d' said the storms here always come in from Narragansett, to the east, so if I wanted to "ride out of the weather," my best bet was to go north towards Woonsocket and into Massachusetts. When I was through with my coffee, I thanked him for his recommendation and followed his advice precisely. In spite of his confidence as a forecaster, however, the rain never stopped.

Twenty-five long miles later, we were greeted by the Governor's welcome sign for Massachusetts and, if anything, it was raining harder. I learned that people in New England don't care so much if they are right or wrong, as long as they *speak with authority*. I stopped at another store somewhere near Whitinsville, bought some ready-to-eat food for dinner, and got directions to Sutton Falls Campground. "Are you sure this is a campground for tenters as well as RVs?, I asked. "Oh yea," he said, "I seen lots of people in tents over there last summer."

He was right, Sutton Falls Campground did have places for tents as well as RVs. As a matter of fact, they had all kinds of spaces, and a bath house and swimming hole too, but one thing they did not have was a manager. The place was "Closed for the Season," and every trailer there was locked down tight as a bug in hibernation for winter. We rode across the bridge at the entrance and I decided to stay there for the night anyway. All I really needed was a place to go to the bathroom, and with no other guests to be offended, I followed Pep's example and took to the woods. With my rain gear still on, I then set up the tent, fed Pep and myself, and crawled into the dryness of the camper before beginning the 4-layer strip down in order to get into my sweat pants. The rain gear would just have to drip on top of my sleeping bag. Cold, damp, and miserable, I drifted off into dreamland, pondering how I could have gone from such luxurious creature comforts at Guy's house to such crude circumstances at Sutton Falls in only 24 hours.

My brother Guy's nice house.

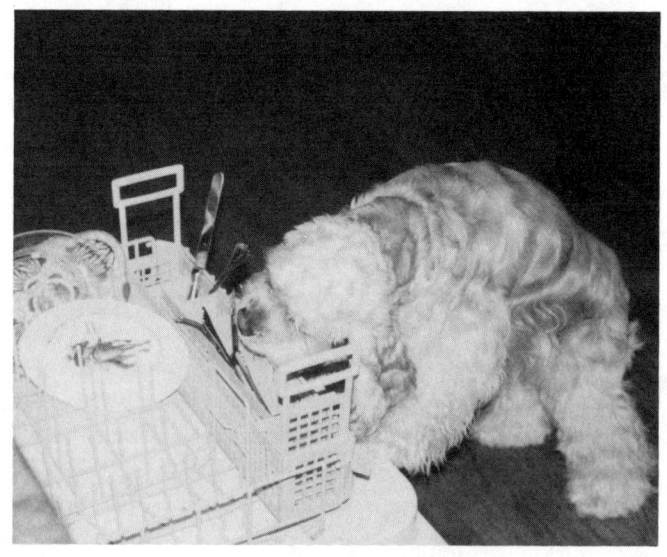

His unusual dishwasher!

Day 26: MASSACHUSETTS

Waking up the next morning at Sutton Falls Campground reminded me of why I liked Colorado so much, or conversely, why I was happy to no longer live in New England. When the weather gets bad here, it can stay that way for a long time. We may have snow in Colorado, or occasionally even rain, but the sun comes out almost every day, and I never remember going more than a whole day, even in the middle of winter, without being blessed by warm golden rays. Today in Massachusetts was just the same as it had been the night before: cold, damp, overcast, with rain and drizzle alternating in a pattern that showed no signs of changing. The mud had gotten so deep at my campsite that I pulled the bike onto the concrete pad next to mine in order to pack up the tent. The denier material was wet but not soaking, and it had continued to keep me dry through the night, faithful to its purpose. Supposedly, everything which might get wet could also dry out later, all we needed was some sunshine, a commodity sorely lacking at this point.

Pep looked like a wet rat as he jumped into his kennel, ready for another day of adventure regardless of the weather. For that matter, I've never seen any precipitation or temperatures which would keep him from wanting to be included in the action, "Go Time." We slithered across the same bridge we had entered over last night and bid Sutton Falls farewell. I'm sure there must be times, in the middle of the summer, when this place is an idyllic vacation spot, but for us, right now, it was a definite "out of here" mind frame.

A very rural back road from the campground lead to a less wooded road and finally, near Westborough, Massachusetts, signs to Interstate 495, an outer limits beltway around the Boston metropolitan area. We had come only about 25 miles when a Krispy Kream Donut Shop jumped out at me and said, "Stop, Come in out of the rain, Have some fresh donuts and Hot coffee here while you Dry out." It sounded so good in my imagination I could not resist. I did everything except the "dry out" portion which would have taken hours. While I was eating breakfast, however, a man came up and asked about the motorcycle and trailer, how far north were we planning to go at the end of October in New England, etc. He was not criticizing me, just showing a genuine concern for whether or not I knew what I was doing. His sincerity was obvious, and I shared with him my plans from here. Then, realizing that I was out of my souvenir photos, I ran out to the motorcycle saddle bag which had the envelope full of extra copies, grabbed another 8 or 10 and, quickly tucking them into a dry spot in my jacket, hurried back to the inside of the restaurant and the friendly soul at my table. He thanked me for the snapshot and gave me his final discouraging piece of advice, "the weather here in New England this time of year can stay rotten for days on end. The closer you are to the coast, the more rain and fog you'll see." Once again, donning my raingear and covering Pep's kennel with his own little waterproof, zip-up vinyl cover, I waved so long to my new weather advisor and got onto Interstate 495. This is also known as the "Blue Star Memorial Highway" along this particular segment which merges with Interstate 95 about 26 miles north of Boston Harbor. Traveling in moderate to heavy rain is slow going on a motorcycle for a lot of reasons, mainly visibility and safety. The rain eventually flows off the windshield due to the force of the wind, but without windshield wipers, it is a gradual process which tends to decrease visibility at best, and obscure it at worst. The safety factor is always important to consider on a motorcycle, but in rainy conditions, when the pavement is slippery and braking ability is reduced, it becomes tantamount to survival. The wind-buffeting and slush-splashing from huge dump trucks and tractor trailers speeding past makes the whole rig unstable. Whether they did it intentionally or not, the drivers came so close that I actually thought they were trying to run me off the road. Which, in fact, they indirectly accomplished when we pulled off at the Chelmsford rest area to try to regain some senses and stamina in this grueling battle to go north. After I had swung my leg over the saddle and turned toward Pep's door, a jolt of fear ran through me. My right saddle bag cover was missing. I looked around the parking lot frantically searching for a blue cover with chrome top rails. It was nowhere to be found. Even Pep joined in the search as I retraced the last few hundred yards from where we pulled in off the highway. Still, there was no top. It was beginning to dawn on me what had happened. When I grabbed these photos back at the donut shop, it was raining and I didn't take the time to close the latches, leaving the cover on the saddlebag by gravity alone. Then when I did come back out, it was still raining, and I didn't recheck every latch before we took off. I had already gone over 130 miles in terrible weather today; some pothole or bump caused the cover to drop off, and I didn't hear it fall. Going back would be a another long hard trip in bad weather to retrace my route, and even if I found the cover, the chances of it not being damaged from trucks running over it were slim indeed. I decided to just lick my wounds, bite the bullet of the replacement expense (probably $100), and go on from here.

A short distance later, we crossed into New Hampshire at Portsmouth, paid the toll road fee to drive 10 miles, and then crossed the bridge over the beautiful harbor, even in a light rain, to the state of Maine on the other side. We would spend much more time in New Hampshire later, but this was the southeast corner where the beaches and seaports are located for the whole state.

I asked the lady at the toll booth how far it was to Freeport and she didn't pause an instant before answering the exact miles to the Portland turnoff and then I-95 to Freeport. "Follow the signs from there to the L.L. Bean Store," she added. It was obvious a whole lot of people had already asked the same question on their way up the coast.

Thankfully, the rain had slowed down to an overcast with mist now, and both Pep and I were able to shed the heavy rain gear. The Maine Turnpike exits were familiar from years of driving to my parent's summer "cabin" in Weld, Maine, the west central part of the state, near the Rangely Lakes region. Kittery, Wells, Kennebunk, Biddeford, and then Portland covered 60 miles.

We veered east to I-95 and arrived in Freeport half an hour later. I had never been to the L.L.Bean store in spite of coming to Maine dozens of times and having been a fan of their sportswear and casual clothing for years. My charge card statements attest to my regular patronage of their good quality merchandise, and I was on the prowl for a new pair of boots, one of their specialties. What I did not realize, however, until I turned into the town of Freeport was how many *other* stores there were in addition to L.L. Bean. Eddie Bauer, Levi's, Benneton, Oneida, Ralph Lauren, Black and Decker, in short, just about every major brand consumer manufacturer was represented in one way or another. Apparently, the drawing power of the L.L. Bean store over the years provided an opportunity for other merchants to take advantage of the affluent traffic, and take advantage they did! I parked in one of the L.L. Bean courtesy parking lots, this particular one designated for "Their Friends with Recreational Vehicles or Trailers." Since it had almost stopped raining completely by now, I tied Pep up to the trailer safety chain, after giving him a good inspection-walk around the grounds, and ambled over to the L.L. Bean Store, a fairly large, one-story building across the street from the parking lot. Then I saw a sign that said this was the "Outlet Store," the main store, with a much bigger selection, was up the hill on Route 1.

There, on the most prominent corner in this small town, the entire northeast quadrant contained a huge building rising up 3 or 4 stories high, made of glass and stone construction with just enough wood to look rustic, complete with the L.L. Bean courtyard and rest area in front. It was definitely the largest sporting goods and accessories store I had ever seen. My impressions were confirmed when I entered the lobby and read that over three million customers a year now visit this establishment started by Granddaddy Bean in the 1920's as a small camping equipment supplier, with an eye toward lasting quality. This sort of place was dangerous for me because they readily accepted every credit card I had, and I knew I could go broke if I did not get out of there fast. My new leather boots are the best I have ever owned, a lace up, ankle height model which is heavy enough for motorcycle riding but comfortable for hiking around in camp or on a trail. A bottle of leather conditioner to go with them, some gift slippers for Sandy, a new chewy bone for Pep, and I was out of there. Whew! Only spent $168 and was I ever relieved.

    I picked up Pep, and we strolled around town enjoying what appeared to be the last precious moments of no rain. Clouds had blown in off the ocean and late afternoon showers appeared to be inevitable. The Freeport Ice Cream Shop also billed itself as providing free information with any purchase, so, under the circumstances, I was forced to buy a butter pecan cone in order to find out how to get to a nearby campground.

    Unlike in Sutton Falls, the Sandy Cedar Haven Campground was bustling with activity, even as it started to rain again. I checked in for a $12 fee, among the highest I paid on the trip, but I was happy to have a place to set up camp before the real deluge began. Fearing the worst back in town, I had purchased a pizza supreme plus a six-pack of John Adams beer to eat inside my tent. Pep's kennel was protected with his waterproof cover, and we were about as comfortable as could be under the (wet) circumstances as we turned in for the night in Bean's town.

Day 27: MAINE

Nothing was more depressing than waking up the next morning in Freeport, Maine. I had heard the rain off and on all night long, and now, at daybreak, it was definitely "on." My Hondaline cover had become super saturated and, unlike the tenting material, it was not heavy enough to withstand continual drenching. My seat was going to be soaking wet too, which meant more raingear today for sure. Almost everything I had was wet or dirty, so I decided to go over to the recreation center near the manager's office to wash and dry some clothes. She had only $3 in quarters which meant I had to ration my washing for 2 loads. The billiard table made a good sorting and folding table, but the roof had a leak in it near the washer and I had to be careful not to get the drips on my laundry as I pulled it out. While I was in there, the door was propped open and I let Pep run around to his heart's content since he could not get any wetter and the concrete floor would not be hurt by a few more muddy paw prints.

As I was finishing up my last load in the washing machine, an older lady came in to do some laundry for her husband and herself. She was very bright, and I enjoyed her conversation more than anything else all day; of course, there was not much competition for pleasant experiences. She said her husband had retired from a medical practice in Canada and that they were on their way over to some town in

New York to visit their daughter and grandchildren. Without being bitter, she explained to me the differences between the health systems in the "states" and Canada. From what she said, most of the Canadian doctors felt their professionalism, especially their patient relationships, had been compromised by the government health care program and that her husband was happy to be retired. It was just too much of a hassle according to him. I also was interested to hear her views on the tax levels for all goods and services: the government was inadvertently encouraging a black market which existed for almost everything. It was one of the most compelling arguments for less government interference in the market place I had ever heard and I told her so. She responded by offering me an extra garbage bag in order to transport my clothes back to my tent without getting them wet. I thanked her for her help under the circumstances and pondered again her remarks. No matter how many things are wrong with our political system in the United States, it was still the most efficient and equitable governance for the greatest number of its citizens.

    If I waited for the rain to stop in Freeport, I might not ever get to leave so, wet and dripping, I packed up as best I could and we sloshed our way back to U.S. Route 1. If the rain had made visibility difficult yesterday, it was even worse today, borderline impossible in my opinion. After only 5.3 miles on my trip odometer for the day, I pulled into The Down East Village Motel and Restaurant in Falmouth to check out their room rates. $48 per night was extravagant for me on this trip, but I was so ready to get warm, dry out, and just plain rest up, that I went ahead. Even though it was only 11 a.m., I laid down on the bed and napped for a couple of hours before waking up, to more rain, of course. A newspaper forecast said tomorrow should be better so at least I still had hope. Everything that could be brought into my motel room was hung up to dry out, including my clothes and sleeping bag, and I caught up on note taking, writing, and some relaxed reading.

That night I called Sandy who was away on a business trip, and, to add insult to injury, she was in Orlando, Florida, where the weather was "warm and sunny, with only slight breezes now and then."

"Sounds really tough, Dear. Just for the record, I'm glad you're not with me right now. You would never go motorcycle riding again if you had experienced the weather I've had for the last two days. It has gotten downright depressing, and I am ready to head back to Colorado." She was pleased to hear me say that, and I promised to be home, "come hell or highwater," before the end of the month. Since this was the 21st day of October, I figured I could keep my word without breaking any speed limits or setting marathon riding records. My only other family visit was to be my aunt and uncle in Kansas City, whom I would call in a couple of days with an exact time of arrival.

That evening, I had the distinct pleasure of meeting another couple from Canada at the Down-East Village Restaurant. The hostess had told them about my adventure (and mishaps), and they ended up asking me to join them at their table for dinner. It seems that the lady was a writer herself and wanted to know all about my trip, what had inspired me to make the journey with my dog, was I having a mid-life crisis, and did I plan to write about my travels? I tried to answer every question she had and they returned the courtesy to my inquiries. He was in the real estate business in

Quebec City and had gone into a joint venture in a Portland rehabilitation project with some other investors, and they were on their way down there to see how things were progressing. Her books had been mainly about antique furniture collecting, but she was ready to try some fiction and would start this winter. Their son and daughter-in-law, and grandchild, lived in Portland so this investment also gave them a business excuse to make a trip they enjoyed making anyway. I told them about my one and only trip to Quebec City, in a small plane, and the nightmarish taxicab ride from the airport to historic downtown with a driver who spoke no English. Even worse, he had only 2 speeds - full speed ahead and full speed sitting on the horn. Women and children jumped back on the sidewalk as the cabby nearly ran them over, oblivious to their safety, or our pleas for mercy. It was the most harrowing ride I had ever experienced, but they said the taxi drivers are notorious for reckless driving in their attempts to squeeze more fares into a day's work. Apparently, unless they actually maim or kill someone, which sometimes happens, the police just look the other way under the assumption that the taxis are *good* for Quebec's tourist business. It was funny now, sharing the stories with them, although at the time I thought *we* might soon be dead.

Since I did not plan on riding anywhere that evening, I had indulged in a few glasses of Chardonay wine, and the man donated his steak scraps to Peppy. They smelled so good when I got back to the motel room I was tempted to chew on them myself before turning them over to Pep, but I was already well fed and full. Then when he started to drool for me at the first sniff of the paper bag, I could not resist his mournful countenance anymore. We both went to sleep that night completely satisfied, with hope and anticipation of dryer and warmer days ahead. Remarkably, that is just what tomorrow had in store.

Three million customers a year can't be wrong.

Time to dry out.

Day 28: NEW HAMPSHIRE & VERMONT

If the sun has ever looked better than it did that morning, I cannot remember the occasion or imagine the circumstances. It was literally heart warming to open the motel door and see the sun coming up on the horizon. I immediately took the cover off the GoldWing to see how wet the seat was and could I tolerate the moisture or would I have to take the sheepskin seat cover off and let it "blow dry" off the end of a trailer side rail. It was not that bad. Everything else was also dry by now, and I could not wait to load up and be heading west again.

Last night I had thought this part of Maine was the northernmost point of my travels in the United States, as well as the most easterly, but when I actually compared the latitude of Freeport, Maine to Missoula, Montana, there was no comparison. Missoula was just below the 47th parallel while Freeport was just above the 43rd. I would have had to drive to northern Maine, say Houlton or higher, to be even with northern Montana. It doesn't appear that way on a map because the map is flat and Maine *looks* so much further north than Montana. In actual fact, a town in Minnesota, Angle Inlet, is the most northern piece of geography in the *continental* United States, Alaska being in a climate and geography all its own.

We traveled down U.S. Route 1 to Portland, enjoying all the small coastal towns we had not taken the time to see on our trip north, once again grateful for the warmth of the sun's rays. The road crossed over Casco Bay and around an old historic section called "Back Cove," full of old colonial houses, each one more charming and unique than the one before. Then we rode west to pick up Route 202, heading southwest to Sanford, Maine and on to the New Hampshire border. Staying on the same road, we came to Concord, the capital of New Hampshire, before lunch time.

The historical marker at the Merrimac River bridge said that settlement in this area had begun in 1659, and in 1733 the village was incorporated as Rumford by *Massachusetts*. After years of dispute, it was determined in 1762 that the area lay within New Hampshire's boundaries, and in 1765 it was reincorporated as Concord. The state capital was moved there in 1808. President Franklin Pierce had a residence in Concord and Mary Baker Eddy, the founder of Christian Science religion, was born nearby. Out west, in Colorado and beyond, most history is measured in terms of the last century; here, in New England, *all* historical plaques relate to times and events at least two hundred, and often three hundred years ago. Twenty miles west of Concord, we turned onto Route 9, continuing a southwest direction toward Keene. More history, beautiful parks, and interesting people greeted us at this last stop in New Hampshire. A few miles further west and we crossed over the Connecticut River separating Vermont from New Hampshire. The fall foliage was still so gorgeous at this river crossing that I stopped to take a picture of the Vermont Welcome Sign. Oddly enough, there were no welcome centers at these secondary road crossings and entryways to a states' borders here in New England. Those (expensive) tourist stops are reserved for major interstates with a continual year round traffic to justify the staffing costs.

Brattleboro, Vermont, on the immediate west side of the river, was the site of Fort Dummer, the first permanent English settlement in 1724. The first European settlement, however, was a French blockhouse constructed on Lake Champlain in 1666, near present day Burlington, Vermont's largest city at only 39,127 population. All of Vermont is lightly populated with a total of 562,000 people ranking it 48th out of 50 states.

Highway 9 soon entered the Green Mountain National Forest, and I enjoyed touring through park-like woods again. A sign pointing north to Mount Snow reminded me of my earliest ski trip recollections as a teenager with my older brother, Larry, and some classmates. It was only a four or five hour drive from southern Connecticut to this part of Vermont and a ski trip was always the highlight of a Spring break or Christmas get-away. Although it was not that far out of my way to visit the ski area, I figured it would be so different after 30 years that I might not recognize the resort. Besides, I once again had that late afternoon prodding of wanting to find a place to stay before dark. A campground in Vermont this time of year was almost out of the question; they were all closed for the season, waiting for Spring and Summer to accommodate campers with sanity. If the signs in the National Forest had not been so specific about prohibiting overnight parking of any kind, I might have been willing to test my sleeping bag warmth once again, but as it was, we rode into Bennington, Vermont about 5:30 that afternoon.

I knew something was wrong as I made my way down the main street of this small New England town that Friday afternoon. Bennington is a college town and apparently this was Homecoming Weekend of one sort or another causing every parent and boyfriend to have rented accommodations weeks and even months ago, according to the proprietor of the Vermonter Motor Lodge. The proprietor, Elle Keegan, tried to be helpful, however, and called a couple of places to see if they had any space. Her second call made a reservation for me at the Hoosick Valley Bed and Breakfast, only 7 miles away.

It was dark when I pulled into the gravel driveway of this old colonial inn with charming hosts, John and Maria. They even offered to let Pep sleep in my room with me, but I had already walked him and he was hooked up to his kennel, on guard. I was even more surprised when I signed the register to see this Bed and Breakfast was rated one of the top twenty in the state of *New York*. I had crossed another state line in the darkness without even realizing it, about 3 miles east of here.

Maria recommended a place to eat dinner called "The Man Of Kent," a pub just down the road owned and run by a transplanted Englishman, also named "John." Even though this was almost two thousand miles away from the Red River Campground in Texas, the atmosphere in the bar was the same. Big John wasted no time in saying hello, serving a frosted mug of "stout" and introducing me to four or five other people at our corner of the bar. Since they were already ahead of me by a number of ale mugs, the conversation was lively from the outset. What a cross section of celebrates! Two young men were just through with work at a part of the National Forest managed by their employer, some giant timber company. The older of the two, still in his twenties, had a degree in forestry, and prided himself in his knowledge of hardwoods, growth rates for timber, and environmental concerns. A couple, who didn't give their names, looked as if they were there on the sly, constantly glancing around to see if anyone they knew was staring at them. Finally, a young man next to me wrote questions for TV quiz shows, and matched trivia with the best of them. His girlfriend of four or five years had recently gone back to Kentucky to live with her parents, and he could not make any sense of their whole relationship. "Why do we have to get married?" he would ask again and again. I confessed to a singular lack of success or knowledge on the sensitive motivations of women in general, which I thought might appease him, but he only drank and postulated all the more. If I had not been on a motorcycle, I might have stayed longer, enjoying the well-lubricated company, but I already was concerned about Pep back at the Inn and wanted to get a good night's sleep myself for the long ride through the rest of upper New York state tomorrow.

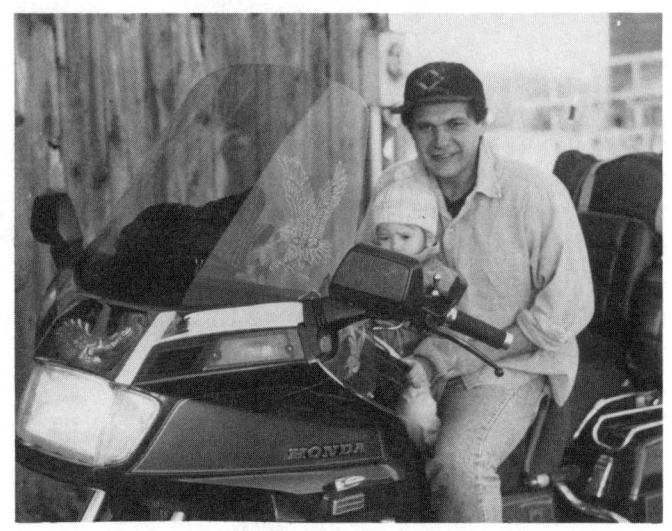

Hang on Dad! Here we go!

Man of Kent, a.k.a. John.

Day 29: NEW YORK

My room at the Hoosick Valley Bed & Breakfast was full of colonial charm. The wide pine plank flooring, an oval braided rug next to my poster bed, and John's original oil paintings of landscape scenes hanging on the walls were a warm sight to wake up to. This was a place where almost any visitor would feel close to home, no matter where they were from. A quick tour outside to let Pep loose and then I was back inside for breakfast after a hot shower. Maria had a small kitchen on the second floor to complement the main one downstairs and two other couples were equally ready for her delicious pancakes and sausage.

It seemed strange to me that although I was still a long way from Colorado, I found myself talking in terms of the end of our journey. It would be a relatively straight shot from the Mid-Atlantic states to the Midwest and on to Denver, so I thought. The wife of a German man seemed especially interested in where we were going so I showed her my traveling map of New York and New England. As she leaned over my shoulder to see where Freeport, Maine was, I made a sweeping motion with my right finger all the way to the coast, and accidentally poked her ample right breast, poised off the edge of the map. Without a moment's hesitation in reply to my statement of that's where the L.L. Bean store is, she said "that's not all that's over there," with a good natured laugh while I stammered an apology. Both couples were on fall outings to visit some relatives and see the New England foliage, a pastime it's hard to grow tired of watching.

Outside Pep had made friends with the Dalmatian dog of John and Maria, who like his owners, seemed only too happy to share hospitality. They romped around a barnyard full of chickens and goats, but what interested Pep the most were the sheep behind a wire fenced pen. I have been told that Border Collies instinctively herd and Pep was just dying to show off his heritage. The sheep were not so anxious to participate, however, and after a couple of snapshots with John and his new baby boy sitting on my GoldWing, we headed west again for Troy and Albany. There, we picked up Interstate 88, a beautiful, well-maintained freeway with gentle curves all the way to Binghamton, New York, 128 miles further west. We were blessed once again with another crisp, clear fall day, perfect for traveling with full leathers, and no rainwear, a weather condition I would never take for granted again. At the picturesque park there, where Pep and I had lunch and chased a few squirrels respectively, a man came up to ask what part of Vermont we were from. Quizzically, I said we were from Colorado as he went over for a closer look at my license tags. They are green just as they are in Vermont, except without the outline of the mountains. He had grown up in Rutland, Vermont and probably just wanted to reminisce a little. I listened attentively as he spoke of doing earth-moving while building the Killington ski resort, and how Vermont's economy really needed the skiers, then as well as now. I told him that resort operators in

Colorado call the snow "white gold" for just the same reason, tourist dollars.

At Binghamton, Interstate 88 merged with Interstate 81, a more north-south route, and an extension of the same highway I had been on in Virginia several days earlier. We cruised down to Scranton, Pennsylvania by early afternoon, and I then spent about an hour trying to find an open campground before giving up and renting a room at the Comfort Inn. They were very strict about no pets in the rooms, however, so Pep was going to have to sleep in his kennel on top of the trailer for two nights in a row, which he was always very good about doing even though his preference is clearly to be on the ground hooked up to his safety chain with the freedom of going in or out at his pleasure. In a motel parking lot at a fairly urban area, though, I felt more comfortable with him being protected and out of sight. Moreover, I could still see his cage on the trailer from my motel room.

Since I had a TV in my room for the first time in many, many nights, I decided to get some chicken wings and a bottle of wine to bring back to the motel for dinner. The manager gave me a copy of a map to the nearest shopping center. While I was turning off a side road and stopped at a red light near the entrance, a muscular athlete on a ten speed bike was blocked at the crosswalk by a man who had inadvertently pulled too far forward with his station wagon before stopping. In a totally uncalled for display of anger, the young man on the bike started pounding on the old man's windows and calling him foul names at the top of his lungs. I watched in amazement as the old man tried to ignore the onslaught and finally pulled ahead before the traffic light changed. The bicycle rider just stayed in the vehicle lane, blocking traffic, yelling "Hey, any of youse guys got any problems?" and challenging anybody who had "any problems" to step out and duke it up with him. Well, I have a policy myself. Whenever someone is 6 feet 2 inches tall, weighs at least 230 pounds, with a build like a New York Giant linebacker, and is at least partially out of his mind, I always agree with him. I could not imagine what was wrong with this guy, but he had proven his mental instability to me beyond a shadow of a doubt. I had no desire to test him further.

      He was gone when I came out of the delicatessen and I would not be surprised if he had been arrested by then for disorderly conduct, although I had not heard any police gun shots, and this maniac was not one to willingly be arrested. I wished I could have introduced him to the Black-Asian Punk Rock Gang in Washington,D.C., just for the entertainment value of a real life "reach out and touch someone" situation. I double locked my motel room that night, just for an extra measure of safety, and went to sleep happy and contented that physical violence was not an everyday occurrence on this trip.

Day 30: PENNSYLVANIA

There was a heavy frost on the ground when I went out to walk Pep in the morning. Thank goodness I was wrapping up my trip rather than just starting out in the northern part of the country. I knew over a month ago, when I was still in the planning stage, that this would be cutting it close to the changes of season, already apparent everywhere. More important than the frost, however, was the clear sky last night. That gave me reasonable assurance of another clear day today, and clear was good, much better than cloudy, no comparison at all. Nevertheless, with the end of October closing in, and ever mindful of my promises to Sandy, I took to the interstates again today. I-81 continued southwest toward Harrisburg, Pennsylvania, the state capital.

About half way between Scranton and Harrisburg is a little town right off the Interstate named "Frackville." Parts of the Appalachian Mountain Range are on both the east and west sides of this little town, and my guess is that coal mining is the biggest part of its legacy. By coincidence, I had nearly run out of gas at this point on the turnpike and pulled in for a pit stop at 9:45 a.m. Sunday morning. As I rode into town on the main street from the highway, I saw block after block of old row houses. They were all 2 story, similar architecture, similar vintage, and in obvious decay after 50 or 60 years of exposure. The 7-11 convenience store met my needs adequately, however, and I would not have thought more about it except the bells started ringing for the Catholic Church directly across from where I was refueling. Several stocky old men were standing outside the church smoking their last few puffs before going inside for the service. They all wore dark polyester suits with heavy black shoes, and white socks. A tie was awkwardly hanging down from a white shirt collar which would not button at the top. Like the homes around them, they too appeared in a bad state of repair, from age and improper care. The only place in the whole town which was shining in splendor was the Catholic Church. It had new copper gutters, new brickwork in the walls, a newly remodeled entryway in matching brick and stone with freshly painted wrought iron railings. The church's sparkling appearance and condition just jumped out at me in comparison to everything else, living or dead, in the town of Frackville.

I refigured my gas mileage and in the last two fill ups I had purchased 4.2 and 4.8 gallons, a total of 9 gallons which had taken Pep, me and the GoldWing 307 miles. This calculated out to 34.1 miles per gallon, on both highway and secondary roads but at mainly cruising speeds in both cases.

We crossed the mighty Susquehanna River at Harrisburg and picked up I-70 for the next 200 miles to the West Virginia line. It was a beautiful afternoon ride and, in the absence of any mandatory stops, I was pleased to be making such good time. The last major town in Pennsylvania, Washington, was only about 20 miles south of Pittsburgh on I-70, but with a Sunday afternoon lull, we never even slowed down for traffic as we entered West Virginia. Wheeling was only 10 miles into the state, and the welcome station had given me the name and exact location of a campground they said was open "year round" near Wheeling.

    The Dallas Pike Campground was indeed open, yes, it had spaces for tents, and hot and cold showers, and it was convenient to the Interstate. What more could I ask for? "Do you have a spot that is a little more level than the side of a hill?" "Level?" he said. "Do you know where you are, mister? You're in West Virginia. There are no level spots in the whole damn state!" He laughed as he cranked out his comments and I could not help but laugh with him. "Well, you wouldn't want me to tip over in the middle of the night, when I rolled around in my sleeping bag, would you?" I asked. He then showed me another spot which came closer to being level, and I told him we could make do with this one. It was also a shorter walk to the rest rooms, which appealed to me with crooked paths in the dark night. I set up camp again, fed Pep and hooked him up to be on guard, and rode about a mile to the Kentucky Fried Chicken outlet near the interstate exit for dinner. West Virginia was all right as far as I was concerned, and it was good to be back in the open air again. Pep felt the same way, I'm sure, as we drifted off to sounds of crickets and night owls.

Day 31: OHIO & KENTUCKY

I had filled up the tank on my GoldWing last night when I went out for chicken, but it was so dark then I did not realize how dirty my windshield was. This morning, as I left the campground, I decided to stop at the same convenience store to clean my windshield. While I was there, a different attendant than the one last night comes out and says "That's enough cleaning. If you're not going to buy any gas, I don't want you using any more of my wiper towels." Perhaps I should have "checked in" with him first, but I knew I still had the receipt in my wallet from the gas and food purchases last night. I took it out to show him, and he did not apologize or say anything, but just waved his hand down at the ground, as if in disgust, and walked back inside. Talk about a problem with the world! I did not know what was wrong with him, but I was sure that anything else I said or did would only aggravate him more, so I finished cleaning my windshield and left.

We were in downtown Wheeling in a matter of minutes and crossing the very commercial Ohio River only a short time after that. At this point in the panhandle, West Virginia is only 12 miles wide. If we had not spent the night at a campground there, we could have blinked and missed the state altogether. My wife was born in this state, near Beckley, so I was happy to have had the story to tell her about no level spot at the campground, which she, too, found amusing.

As we crossed the Ohio River, however, West Virginia became history, and the beautiful rolling hills of Ohio awaited our journey today. We had covered 347 miles yesterday so I felt as if we were making good time in my commitment to be home before the end of the month and wanted to ride at least another 300 miles today.

One stop I really wanted to make, however, was the Honda factory in Marysville where all the GoldWings are made. When I asked at the Ohio Welcome Center about visitors' hours at the Honda plant, the "welcome lady" said "they no longer offer open tours to regular people, just special situations." Well, I knew that I was a "special situation," but the question was did *they* know I was a special situation. I thought about that as I rode toward Columbus, right next to Marysville. What would happen if I just rode up to the plant? Some guard would probably ask if I had an appointment with someone, and what was the mucky muck's name. Could I convince him I was somebody "special?" Probably not, I decided. They could have GoldWing riders trying to stop in at the plant every day during the summer and turn them away so as not to interfere with production. Who was I to ask for an unscheduled visit? Maybe I'll make the 25th anniversary rally here and get to see the factory then.

In spite of being scorned by the Honda people, I really enjoyed my ride through Ohio. The weather was beautiful (translation: dry), the highways were in good shape, and the rolling terrain on a fall afternoon made a delightful combination for enjoyable touring. A trucker asked if he could take our picture at a rest area so he could show his wife not all motorcyclists are "bad dudes." He said that she loved Border Collies and would be very interested in my story. Of course, with that kind of praise, I had to give him a souvenir photograph as well. He also forewarned me about all the construction in progress in Cincinnati, but I did not realize just how bad it was going to be. If I took a more northerly route to Saint Louis, I would miss Kentucky altogether, and I didn't want to do that.

My timing for Cincinnati could not have been worse. We reached the Interstate 275 beltway about 4:30 in the afternoon and the construction detours were diverting traffic *through downtown* and not around it on the beltway, due to worse delays on the bypass route. (Although I do not see how any other route could possibly have been worse.) We crawled through downtown in rush hour traffic on I-71, which had almost become a giant parking lot. I have been on the Long Island Expressway leaving New York City and this was exactly the same speed, slow and stop. Then we crossed the Ohio River again, going into Kentucky, and it was even more grueling. Three lanes of interstate had to be merged into one lane due to the construction and, almost unbelievably, it was on the ascent of one of the famous seven hills of Cincinnati. Stop and crawl on a steep uphill grade for a motorcycle and trailer is really tiring. Every time I would start to release the clutch and inch forward, I would have to stop to put on *both* the hand brake and the rear foot brake because of the steep grade. When we finally got to the top of that hill, I pulled off to the Kentucky Welcome Center, not for information, but to take an honest to goodness fall-down type rest. I was totally exhausted from the 2 hours of gridlock combined with my own nervousness from all the truckers and dusty construction. The good news was that the General Butler State Park was only a few more miles down the road.

General William Orlando Butler was a hero in the War of 1812, and the park was full of historical mementoes and nineteenth century folklore. We rented a campsite near a big, scenic lake, in which Pep took his usual swim, but I opted for a hot shower in the well furnished community wash rooms. I cleaned up before going over to the main lodge for dinner so that I could be decent for the dining room, and also be ready to ride first thing in the morning. The foliage here was well past its prime and the night-time sky scared me with its lack of clarity.

Day 32: INDIANA & ILLINOIS

The morning brought with it much better weather than I had feared last night. It was not exactly sunny, but it surely was not overcast and rainy either. I had a reasonable basis for expecting the day to improve as we traveled, and lo and behold, that is exactly what happened. A short ride from Carrolton, Kentucky put us back on Interstate 71 heading south for Louisville.

The construction work outside Cincinnati yesterday afternoon was a harbinger of what to expect on all the roads in Kentucky. Even the interstates were being patched up with traffic funneling into one lane while blacktop was applied to the other. My first real job during the summer while I was a college student had been working on a blacktop crew so I knew how hard and hot that work can be. Even in the relative coolness of fall rather than summer, the steam still comes off the back of the dump truck as it drops a combination of molten tar and gravel at over 200 degrees Fahrenheit. The blacktop must be applied while it is hot because that is when it is also malleable, conforming its final shape to that of the road cavities to be filled. My particular job had been that of a tamper, the guy who pounds each square foot by hand in hopes of making a permanent bond where the power roller cannot be used. I never had any trouble going to sleep at night when I got through working on that blacktop crew all day and, by the looks of the sweat on these workers' brows, they deserved to be tired at day's end too. In spite of my best efforts to avoid the freshly tarred spots, I could still hear the gravel flipping up against the GoldWing's fenders long after we had passed by the construction.

Louisville was my third and final crossing of the Ohio River. Although it mat have been the same water each time, the river had a distinctly different appearance in Louisville than it had in either Wheeling or Cincinnati. The combination of boats mixed with commercial river traffic in Louisville was more pleasing to the senses than just the barges and tug boats in Wheeling. All the efforts to reduce pollution in the river seemed to be making a real difference here and the people of Kentucky should be proud of the results.

New Albany, Indiana, the first town on the west side of the bridge over the Ohio River, did not have a welcome center anywhere that I could see from Interstate 64 so we just kept on riding. I could see from the map that Hoosier National Forest was only about 45 miles down the road, and we ended up stopping there for a good walk in the rest areas. While we were there, I met a man from St.Louis, a professional dog handler, who was on his way to Lexington, Kentucky with as beautiful a German Shepherd as I had ever seen in my life. Not only was this dog well-muscled and majestic looking, he behaved impeccably. When his master said "heel," the big dog acted immediately to drop back to the man's left knee. Even Peppy's natural curiosity was not enough to make this animal waver from his handler's command. The German Shepherd's coat was of long hair, smooth and glossy, with a mixture of brown and black handsomely combined. What really surprised me, however, was the man said he had imported this dog from Germany specifically for the

Lexington Police Department, to whom he was delivering the dog now, at a price of $4,000! Apparently it is not unusual for a well bred and well trained Shepherd to be worth that to a Canine Police Unit.

We stopped for lunch at the "Depot Cafe" in Griffin, Indiana, right next to a rusty, single-line railroad track that had undoubtedly seen better days. Although I usually tried to time our breaks so that I was eating in restaurants during the off-peak hours, this day I was hungry early, right at noon. As I sat down in this cafe, it was obvious that most of the customers were "regulars." They knew the waitress by name, the menu by heart, and they sat with other men who also were locals, mainly farmers. The walls were filled with jokes and cartoons about old tractors, older mules, and the fickleness of the weather. While I waited for my "Depot burger," however, the one most amusing to me said, "Please Lord, let there be another Oil Boom. I promise not to piss it away this time." I don't know when the last oil boom was in southern Indiana, but by the looks of the Depot Cafe, and its customers, that prayer had been on the wall for quite a while. Still, the idea of negotiating with God over the preconditions for the next happening of wealth made me laugh.

Five miles west of Griffin, Indiana, we crossed the Wabash River and entered Illinois. I was making good time on I-64 and was deeply grateful, once again, to have a beautiful day for riding. The temperature was in the 60s, and with full leathers, including my heavy gauntlet gloves, I could not have asked for better conditions at nearly the end of October. It was 140 miles to East Saint Louis, and the distance flowed by as quickly as any on the whole trip. Not much to see, less reason to stop, and we reached the huge golden arch, "Gateway to the West," at about 5:30 that afternoon.

      Saint Louis, Missouri during rush hour was not even close to Cincinnati in terms of traffic or delays. A little construction was going on, but it did not interfere with the masses of motor vehicles on the freeways and bridges. We entered Missouri and I finally felt as if I was on the last lap of my journey. Tomorrow night I would be in Kansas City, with my aunt and uncle, and only the state of Kansas left between Colorado and me. Of course, like most plans and schemes of mice and men, they don't work that simply. I didn't have a clue how miserably hard that last stretch was going to be as Pep and I went to sleep that night in Weintzville, Missouri.

Day 33: MISSOURI

A gray overcast sky greeted us outside the "El Cheapo" Motel on the Interstate 70 frontage road. We were 30 miles west of St. Louis, and it was a straight 225 miles to Kansas City. I wasn't worried so much about being able to make it to my aunt and uncle's house as I was about whether this could be the beginning of another storm system moving in. The longer I rode, the more my fears were compounded. The towns passed by in fairly rapid succession: Columbia, home of the University of Missouri, a turn off for Jefferson City, the state capital, and then later, Independence, birthplace and life-long home of Harry Truman. I always felt good about Kansas City. Since I had graduated from high school there, it was almost like coming home again. Home or not, however, the last time Sandy and I had driven back for a reunion I had gotten so lost trying to find my uncle's house, I thought we were in another country. At one point, driving down a street named Troost Avenue, in a terribly run down part of town, she said I reminded her of Chevy Chase in the movie "Vacation," where they had gotten off the highway in St.Louis and ended up in a ghetto. This time was different though. I stayed on I-70 and then I-71 until it intersected with Broadway and followed that major thoroughfare south to the Country Club Plaza, the granddaddy of suburban shopping centers, decorated in a Spanish motif with statues and fountains on almost every corner. Actually, the corners are more like rounded circles, all well maintained and bursting with good taste from classic design. I cannot really afford the Brooks Brothers clothing stores or the Gucci leather shops, but I love to admire the fountains and architecture all the same. It is timeless in its appeal to me, especially with glimmers of intermittent sunshine threading their way through the clouds.

I rode past the Pembroke Hill School, my old alma mater, and on up the Ward Parkway, a residential boulevard whose 1920s mansions seem to get bigger every time I come back to Kansas City. They must all be at least 10,000 square feet with slate roofs and cobblestone driveways leading up to Tudor monster homes with 4 and 5 car garages. How could one family live in something so huge? It's the same question which always crosses my mind, especially when my wife says she wants one. "I'm into gaudy. I can handle that. It's just my style," she jokingly maintains, as if we are going to run right out and plunk down 5 or 10 million to buy one.

Very soon after millionaire's row, I turn onto Brookside Boulevard, and in a few more blocks, I arrive at their home. Both come running out of the house to see my motorcycle rig and, of course, Peppy. They have a huge black Newfoundland dog in the yard who bellows out his disapproval at being excluded from the festivities and excitement, particularly when another dog is involved. His 90 pounds would dwarf Pep, and to be honest about it, he sort of pushes me around too. My uncle said he has had to stop walking "Buckshot" because he was no longer sure who was walking whom. The big Newfy seeing a squirrel could ruin Uncle Bob's whole day, to say nothing of his pair of pants.

Missouri

My aunt has collected antiques ever since I have known her, about thirty some odd years, and she started long before that. Their house is so full of furniture and decorative accessories that turning around too quickly can cause an accident. I will never understand how Buckshot can make it through the hallways without causing major damage. Nevertheless, they invited both Pep and me in for a stay, and we were only too happy to oblige, especially with a sprinkle of rain starting up again. I covered the GoldWing for the night, had a thoroughly enjoyable dinner with my aunt and uncle, and read the weather forecasts over and over in an attempt to plan my strategy for tomorrow. Colder temperatures with freezing rain and drizzle were moving in from the East. "Kansas City is overdue for some heavy precipitation," said my uncle, who sort of prides himself on being knowledgeable about the weather patterns, a regular Farmers' Almanac with just the news I did not want to hear at this point in my trip.

Peppy unwinding.

Waiting out the storm.

Day 34: KANSAS

The nasty weather had not yet fully arrived when we had breakfast at 6 a.m. I had asked my aunt to move it up a little earlier than normal so I could get an early start on the long ride across Kansas, hopefully ahead of any real bad storm. The forecast was still the same, however: increasing winds with clouds and rain as the day went on, storm system moving from east to west. Rather than a relaxed visit as I had planned, it was pretty much eat, sleep, eat, and run from the wonderful hospitality in Kansas City with some of my favorite relatives. They understood what I was trying to do, though, and encouraged me not to take any chances. "If the storm catches up with you, promise me you'll stop and call us from a motel," which I agreed to.

Their yard has some super frisky squirrels so Pep probably would have preferred to stay longer, but we pulled out early that Thursday morning with my uncle providing me a car escort for the "easy way" to get back on the interstate heading west to Kansas. I dutifully followed him into the middle of a construction zone downtown where even he, after living in Kansas City for over 50 years, could not find a way to get on I-70 heading west. He finally pulled off the side of the road in despair, and I said good-bye to both of them before getting on the turnpike going east, the wrong direction, but knowing I could always turn around at the first open exit. It worked fine and I was at the Kansas

Welcome Center sipping a second cup of coffee within 20 minutes after leaving the labyrinth downtown.

The "welcome lady" said it was 400 miles to Colby, Kansas and they, too, were expecting a storm before the afternoon was over. Right now the wind was just starting to blow a little harder, about 10 to 15 knots, and it was drizzling off and on. Outside, It looked much darker to the east than it did ahead on the horizon. I took off and cranked up the GoldWing as fast as I safely could, about 75 miles an hour, and we were flying toward western Kansas.

The Kansas Turnpike took us all the way to Topeka, and then we continued west on I-70 while the turnpike headed south west to Wichita. I had lunch near Salina, Kansas still grateful to be riding on semi-dry pavement and making darn good time to boot. Russell, home of Senator Bob Dole, breezed by about 2:30, Oakley, home of Annie, about 5 p.m., and by 6:30, just when it started to rain pretty hard, we were checking in to the Ramada Inn in Colby, Kansas, and damned glad to be there. I had ridden 405 miles in one super fast day, but I had outrun the storm and with that I was well pleased.

It rained all night, so it seemed, but with only 60 miles to the Colorado border, I felt we were almost home and I could make it the last stretch one way or another, meaning fast or slow, but still riding home. Wrong! The temperatures were dropping as the rain became freezing rain, and by morning I could hardly *walk* across the parking lot much less crank up the motorcycle.

Day 35: WESTERN KANSAS

I was so shaken, and afraid, at the prospect of trying to ride on the ice that I decided to go back into the Ramada Inn Coffee Shop, where I had just checked out, to have another cup and reconnoiter what my choices were. The front desk clerk said that the highway patrol was advising travelers to stay home if at all possible. They were working on sanding and salting the major roads but it would take all day. Current temperature was 24 degrees Fahrenheit with northerly winds at 25 miles per hour, gusting 35 to 40. The weather had clearly caught up with me.

Perhaps I had waited too long into the fall to make my cross country trip. Until today, however, I had really had only 3 terrible days (and 1 horrendous night) out of 35, not too bad a ratio, regardless of the time of year. What to do now is the question. I could stay at the Ramada another day to see if it warmed up enough to melt any ice allowing me to proceed home. Or, I could try to ride slowly down the highway hoping for more sunshine as we got higher in altitude into Colorado. Everybody knows that the sun shines almost every day on the Front Range. The thought of just waiting around in Colby, Kansas for the weather to improve just did not seem practical. Suppose I waited for 2 or 3 days and it was still cold? It could be March before it ever really warms up! I could call Sandy to see if she could rent a trailer to pull behind our truck so that she could drive over to come get me and the bike for the last 200 miles to our home. That would be a last resort because she was working today, Friday, October 28th, and I did not want to worry her or cause her to neglect her business obligations on account of my predicament.

I decided to at least give riding a try. It had to be better on I-70 than it was in the Ramada Inn parking lot, although by 10 a.m. they had done some scraping and sanding there as well. The GoldWing would not start. It clicked and whirred just as it had in Yellowstone over a month ago. I tried again with precisely the same results. It jumped to life on the third attempt and warmed up in a matter of minutes, while I again searched for every piece of warm clothing I could put on. I threw a blanket in with Pep so he could nestle inside his kennel, which was facing backwards, away from the wind. Even as I tried to ride out of the parking lot, I could feel the motorcycle jerk sideways from the gusts of wind pushing the tires across patches of ice. I dared not pull my feet up on the riding pegs for fear I would need them on the ground to keep the bike from tipping over. It was even worse than I had imagined, but I was now going up the ramp to the interstate where I was sure the traction would be better. The highway department had sanded every other 10 feet creating a patchwork of slide-and-go. Perhaps this is an efficient way of keeping 4 wheeled vehicles from slipping out of control, but for the motorcycle and trailer, it was pure hell. As the 2 wheels of the bike would start to slide sideways from the wind, the trailer would act as a sort of brake by being on the sanded part of the highway. When the trailer slipped, the bike had then reached a sanded patch for semi-traction. I pulled off the road only 600 yards from the entry ramp. Could I park the bike and walk back to the motel? What would happen to my motorcycle and trailer if some vehicle slid into it on the shoulder? There was no way to turn around since all traffic was westbound on this side of I-70.

Just then, I looked down the guard rails and saw a sign that said "Roadside Rest Area 4 Miles Ahead." The wind and cold were cutting into my neck, I was shaking with fear over my bike's instability, but I was not going to abandon the rig on the side of the road. I decide to ride down the shoulder to the rest area where I could pull off and regroup. At 5 to 6 miles per hour, I reached the rest area in 45 minutes, cold, shaken, discouraged, and yet, glad to be alive. The phone was out of order and the only communication was a weather radio loudspeaker which kept repeating the dismal forecast: "Travel advisories are in effect. Western Kansas is experiencing a severe cold front, winds gusting up to 50 miles per hour, with a strong chance of snow in the afternoon. Roads are icy and hazardous. Avoid travel if at all possible."

I had no way to avoid travel now. My only question was, "What is the best way and where do we go from here?" I was finally ready to give up on two wheels at this point. If I could find a way to get to a U-Haul Center, maybe I could rent a van-type truck, ride the motorcycle and trailer inside it, and *drive* the last 190 miles to home.

About this time, a couple in a small Nissan sedan pulls up to use the rest rooms at the Arctic Waystation, I mean Colby Rest Area. They didn't really care so much about me, but like most people on the trip, they were concerned about Peppy, whom I ordered to look as forlorn and destitute as possible on hopes of evoking sympathy from someone. Dick and Renata Johnson looked at Pep and me, had a little conference among themselves, and then Dick came over to see if we needed any help. I told him our situation and he immediately said they wanted to help us get to a truck rental place and would give *both Pep and me* a ride to Goodland, Kansas. We got to know each other pretty well during that ride, and I thanked them over and over for their Good Samaritan kindness to two highway vagabonds.

The U-Haul office in Goodland was a one room cubicle staffed by a 60-year-old lady in her bedroom slippers standing next to a Franklin stove. She was not alone, however; there were about 10 to 12 cats curled up or stalking all over the piles of newspapers and old contracts all over the floor. Dick and I just stood there inside the doorway because there was hardly room to turn around much less sit down. She did not have any big trucks for rent but made a couple of phone calls, and some national center directed us to Limon, 110 miles down the road. She then said that Limon "used to be half-way to Denver," but she didn't think it was that far anymore. Was one of the towns moving along over time? I never understood what she was trying to say, but Dick and I both had a good laugh talking about it back in the car.

A couple of hours later, and $168 dollars poorer, I had a 24 foot U-Haul van and was on my way back to the Colby, Kansas rest area to pick up my GoldWing and trailer. It was now about 4 p.m. and I was quickly running out of daylight, since it was still overcast and bitter cold. I bought 200 feet of rope, at the new Wal-Mart in Colby, and returned to the motorcycle to find everything still in tact and undisturbed. Unhooking the trailer, I rode the bike up the narrow loading ramp into the back of the truck. Then, with the skill of a spider, I tied the front wheel to one set of cleats in the front of the cargo area. Next, I looped the crash bars to the side cleats, the seat and back rest to the hooks above that, and the back frame bars to the other side cleats. This bike was not going to move if I had anything to do with it! Another 100 feet of rope for a similar treatment on the trailer and we were on our way down I-70, warm and comfortable inside a U-Haul truck cab. Even Pep seemed pleased at our new transportation arrangements as we pulled into the Western Motor Inn, Burlington, Colorado that night at 7p.m., too exhausted to drive any further, but deeply thankful for the warmth of a motel room to provide shelter from the elements.

10,188 miles, one way or another!

Traveling Buddies - Journey's End!

Day 36: COLORADO HOMECOMING

The temperature at 6 the next morning in Burlington, Colorado made yesterday seem like a heat wave. The restaurant manager said it was 9 degrees on the official town thermometer, and the winds had died down to only 10 to 15 miles per hour. It felt so cold I was not sure even the truck would start, but it did. We pulled out on to the highway without a hint of skidding and rolled west to Limon before stopping for a second cup of coffee. Pep sat right up front in the cab, looking all around as we drove along, just like he was another person riding shotgun.

We turned off Interstate 70 past Limon and headed due west on Highway 86, exactly the same road we had come down going the other way 36 days ago. I was so excited my heart was pounding with anticipation at the prospect of seeing Sandy again, and being safely home. The sun was finally coming out as we passed through Kiowa and Elizabeth to Franktown, only 8 miles from home! I called Sandy from the U-Haul truck center in Parker and she came down to welcome us back and help with transporting any bulky items, like Pep. He was so glad to see her again he almost jumped out of his skin as he took a flying leap into the back of our Jimmy. She took a picture of the bike all tied down in the back of the U-Haul and of Pep and me in front of our trailer which I had already skidded down the ramp.

The manager of the rental center helped me off-load the motorcycle, and then, after I had checked the truck in and Sandy had left to go home, he asked me if I was going to be able to make it home all right. It was about 3 miles to our house in the Pinery and, at noon, the temperature had risen to about 45 degrees. I looked at him in disbelief that even a seventy-year-old man could ask such a question. "Mister," I said, " I've come over 10,000 miles on this motorcycle, all over the country through 42 states including the District of Columbia; I've ridden through wind and rain, and freezing cold ice storms last night in Western Kansas; if I can't make from here to the Pinery, you'd better call the undertaker right now, because I'd have to be dead not to ride these last three miles on this beautiful fall day." "Okay, okay," he said with finality.

I thanked him for his voice of concern and waved good-bye, just as I had done so many times in the last month. But as I looked back, I could see he was wondering whether or not I had all my marbles. I didn't want to give him the satisfaction but, of course, the answer is probably not. It is wonderful to be just a little bit crazy; otherwise I might not have ever taken the trip to begin with and that would have cut out part of my soul. *Travels with Peppy* has indeed been the adventure of my lifetime, and I was thrilled to have completed it, one way or another.